the
Balanced Entrepreneur

the
Balanced Entrepreneur

A Guide to Creating a Purposeful Life and Living it Unapologetically

ESSICA DENNIS

Columbus, Ohio

The Balanced Entrepreneur: A Guide to Creating a Purposeful
Life and Living it Unapologetically

Published by Gatekeeper Press
2167 Stringtown Rd, Suite 109
Columbus, OH 43123-2989
www.GatekeeperPress.com

ISBN (hardcover): 9781642375602
ISBN (paperback): 9781642375589
eISBN: 9781642375671

Printed in the United States of America

For all the women who have supported me, encouraged me, partnered with me, and trusted me. My wish for you is that you never stop pursuing your dreams on the path to your most balanced, purposeful life.

Contents

Letter to the Reader

FRIEND, FIRST I want to thank you for picking up this book. It seems surreal that you've found your way here and I'm truly humbled and honored that this book is sitting in your hands. I've thought about you the entire time I was writing it. I've wondered where you are in your journey and in your life. I've contemplated the thoughts and feelings that keep you up at night, the things that cause you to act and the ones that cause you to stop. I've wondered about what gifts you possess and what your unique purpose is here on earth. But mostly I've thought about the similarities in our journeys and how we're both here to lead exceptional, purpose-filled, balanced lives.

My hope as you pick up this book is that you're searching for something more or following a calling deep inside you that's telling you not to settle. My hope is that you already know you're meant for something great, something bigger than where you are now and the life you're leading today. I also hope your life is already great. Life doesn't have to be broken in order to seek more. Quite the opposite, in fact. I think it's when we experience richness and fullness that we get a taste for what we're meant to have, the life we were created to lead.

I am blessed to have had this stirring for greatness within

me since childhood. My parents said I had a strong intuition and maybe that's what it's called, but for me it felt bigger than that. I've always felt very connected to something much larger than myself. I've never doubted that I was called for something great. When I was in college, I remember telling my roommate during freshman year that I was going to leave a mark; I was going to change the world in some way. I'll never forget her reaction because she just looked at me, perplexed and confused, but also full of love. She believed me but what she said next I'll never forget. She said she didn't feel the same way; she'd never felt that way, never had a stirring inside her that she was made for something great. Her response baffled me and I spent many years contemplating what she'd said. I've wondered if some people are meant for greatness while others aren't, or if I had something special that she lacked.

Today I can confidently tell you that we're all created for greatness. If I am, so are you. It just can't happen any other way. I've been blessed to understand this truth and I need to share the message with others. Call it God, The Universe, The Spirit, source energy; it lives inside us and all around us. It is meant to guide us, encourage us, support us, and walk beside us through this life. For me it is God and you will hear throughout this book how my faith and God have transformed my life. This book is a gift from God. He walked beside me the entire time I wrote it, all the way until the very end when my mouse died and I prayed it would work again because I couldn't imagine editing this entire book without a working mouse! He was there and fixed my mouse with one single prayer and guided the words you will find on the following pages.

You may have a different explanation for that stirring inside of you. That's OK; just listen to it. It's there for a reason. When the world tells you to just be happy with what you have and grateful for every blessing you've received, take the advice; but understand there's more. That stirring is a gift and no one else can tell you it's right or wrong or even what it says or means. That's your job to decipher. My stirring has led me on a wild ride through entrepreneurship when it didn't always make sense to most people, through multiple businesses and up to this book. I will be forever grateful that I didn't stop searching and seeking or I wouldn't be here, following my purpose and walking with you in your journey.

This is the book I wish I'd had when I was twenty-five years old, starting my first company and then at twenty-eight starting my second, and so on and so forth. The world is full of noise and everyone has an opinion, but the voice I so wished I had listened to the most was my own. We all have the answers right inside of us; we just need to learn how to slow down, listen, and act. This book is about finding your greatness, the "more" you were created for, in a balanced way. I will refer to this "more" throughout the book as the thing that lights you up. That dream, vision or idea that makes your heart flutter with excitement while simultaneously feeling a deep sense of inner peace.

This book is about entrepreneurship because that's been my path and it's the best one I've found to create the life of your dreams. It's also about cultivating an entrepreneurial mindset, because wherever you are in life, that's what it's going to take to create the life of your dreams and become a balanced entrepreneur.

As a path, entrepreneurship is not just about running businesses. It's about being the entrepreneur of your life, of your journey. Business is a walk in the park compared to the task of engineering your life to live your best version of it. The goal is to build the life you want to live while simultaneously enjoying the present life you're creating—that's balance. The illusion of "someday," or even retirement, is gone. Most people are unwilling to live the majority of their lives working hard to finally get to retirement and only then start enjoying their lives. This is a great thing! We shouldn't live our lives that way. You can absolutely, and should absolutely stop at nothing to create the life today that you want to live every single day because there are no guarantees.

This book is about balance in designing your life because I don't believe a great life can be lived without it. While you might be tempted to think of my use of the term "balance" as work/life balance, I want to eliminate that idea all together. Work/life balance is far too simplistic and implies that work and life must be equal to offset each other. This is a very narrow view of balance and one I do not subscribe to. So, I am going to introduce you to a new paradigm. When I refer to balance throughout this book, I'm talking about all the critical areas that make up your life. These areas can include career/purpose; family/marriage; health: mental, physical, emotional and spiritual; money; faith/spirituality; hobbies/passions; community/friendships and personal growth/learning.

As a visual, imagine you as the balanced entrepreneur at the center and all of these critical areas surround you. At different times in your life, these areas may grow larger in their importance during any given season, but they are always being balanced among all the others. If at any point one area is taking up too much space in our lives, we simply check back to see what areas have fallen in priority and realign by shifting where we spend our time. Our lives will be shaped by all the decisions we make on a daily basis to keep these critical areas in balance, starting with how we spend our time, which has a massive impact over our lifetimes.

There are many aspects that make up our lives and they can't be summed up as simply work and life. Throughout my journey, this idea of balance has come back over and over again and when I've been the most fulfilled, it's because I've prioritized various key areas to achieve balance. The same is true for when I've been the least fulfilled—those times I've made the mistake of focusing too greatly on only one or two areas, which has caused imbalance. We're going to talk about living your best life in the context of balance because the goal at the end of a life isn't to be the "most successful loser," meaning you're rich in one area while poor in others. The goal is to live in richness and fullness in all the areas of your life and in order to do this, we need to prioritize them, starting right now.

I look forward to sharing my journey with you in the following pages. I've experienced my fair share of ups and downs, but I've learned through all of them. My hope is that my story supports you in your journey. The only thing I ask is that you stay with me until the end. One of my favorite chapters is the very last one, "The Final Game Changers," but I don't believe you'll receive its full benefit without the others. You're in the right place and you've picked up this book for a reason, so let's dive in!

—Jess

INTRODUCTION

The Moment Everything Changed

I WAS LYING ON my back, staring at the ceiling. I imagined the earth supporting my body as I ran my fingers through the worn carpeting. Time stopped. As I looked up at the ceiling, I tried to process the news I had just received. I knew my entire life had changed but my brain couldn't process the news. Intuitively, I felt the flood of emotion coming and yet I knew this was the line—the before and after. I was leaving my life before the news and I was entering my life after.

That's how it always begins for me. Even when I don't see the shift coming, I typically recognize it when I'm lying on the floor because of having the urge to feel close to the earth, to feel grounded. These moments usually come right after or during a breakdown, and right before a breakthrough. It's not a conscious decision to lie down on the floor. Rather, I'm surprised when I find myself there. How did I get here? What am I doing on the floor? I often wonder. They're moments of complete and total surrender, moments of, *I can't take it anymore and I don't know what to do.* They're moments when I don't have the answers and they often involve tears, lots and lots of tears. I can now look back and see them as gifts, but at the time, that's not at all how they feel. They are the breaking points, the critical moments. They feel anything but good, but they're necessary to make a major shift.

This particular moment on the floor was going to change everything. I didn't know it at the time but it was going to change how I viewed work, retirement, time with family, and the necessity to pursue my purpose.

This day was July 18, 2014. I was thirty-one years old. My husband and I had recently moved into our second home and welcomed our second daughter into our family. I had sold my first company, was in the process of growing my second and had just started a third.

As I arrived home that day and pulled into our garage, I received two calls in a row from my dad. Dad and I are close. We see each other every week on Sunday nights for family dinners. I never hesitate to call him and, in fact, we text one another often. That's why receiving a call from him was not out of the ordinary and certainly not cause for alarm. When I saw my phone light up and my dad calling, I decided I would call him back as soon as I was in the house. As I unpacked my car and brought everything in, I was reaching for my phone when he called again. I answered, feeling a bit off balance having received two calls in a short period of time, which was unusual, even for him.

"Hello?" I answered.

"Jessica, it's your father." His statement felt formal and immediately caused me to me to stop what I was doing and pay full attention. The casual call I assumed I was receiving felt different, urgent.

"Yes?"

"Something's happened. It's Erik. He was staying at his mom's this weekend and she went to wake him up this morning . . . ," he trailed off. A long pause followed. I interrupted the silence as panic rose in my voice. "What!?" I shouted. My head was spinning. I started sweating. As he composed himself, he simply said, "He didn't wake up."

I didn't understand.

"What do you mean, he didn't wake up?!" Now I was really yelling. The voice that came out of me was angry, emotional. It didn't feel like my own. The whole situation felt like it was happening around me, to someone else. Not to me.

"He didn't wake up Jess; he's gone. Erik died this morning."

I couldn't process what he was saying. It didn't make any sense. My palms began to sweat and numbness crept in from my toes up through my stomach and eventually transformed into a humming in my ears. I was suddenly completely aware of my surroundings; the blood as it pulsed through my body, the hum of the overhead fan, and the cars driving by outside. He talked about some details that needed to happen and we hung up. No "I love you" or "It's all going to be OK." Just "goodbye" and we hung up.

As I stared at my phone, the most unrecognizable, heart-wrenching pain filled me up and I screamed and fell to the floor. No one was home with me. No one was receiving this news with me and no one was there to hold and comfort me. I lay on the floor screaming, crying, and rolling from side to side. If you've ever experienced this kind of pain, you know what this feels like. This news, this realization that my older brother had died at thirty-five years old in his sleep, was physically painful. My whole body hurt, and I was incapable of holding myself up. The headache started almost immediately and didn't subside for weeks. The pounding behind my raw, red eyes and the nausea in my stomach became unwelcome houseguests who wouldn't leave.

That's how I found myself on the floor, staring at the ceiling, contemplating my entire life. But I'll get back to that in a moment.

The next few weeks went by at a snail's pace. I spent a lot of time lying on the floor, being supported by the earth because it was the only thing that felt reliable, consistent, and trustworthy. We planned and carried out Erik's funeral and hoped we were doing what he would have wished. We didn't know how he wanted his funeral to go because that wasn't a conversation we'd had yet. This wasn't the plan. He was my older brother, my dad's only son, my little girl's fun Uncle Erik. This wasn't how the story was supposed to go.

But that is life. It can be taken in an instant, without warning.

Seeing Things From a New Perspective

Erik wasn't sick; nothing was wrong; he simply passed away peacefully in his sleep for no reason that we were able to discover. He was just gone one day, unexpectedly. I share how he died because it matters. We can wrap our heads around something like cancer, as cruel and undiscerning as it is. We understand that tragedies occur and we can make peace with old age. As humans, we're meaning makers. We seek answers and we need to understand why things happen. The most difficult part of Erik's death was that it left us with unanswered questions that persist to this day. We still don't understand why he died. But even though it doesn't make sense, that doesn't change the outcome.

This tragedy changed my outlook on life in such a profound way. As I lay on the floor, taking in the news of Erik's death, I began to take in the frailty of human life. The earth was supporting my body. My body that was very much alive, my brain swimming, trying to process, my heart racing and simultaneously aching and my legs, tingling, too weak to support my body. And my older brother, the one who told me ghost stories growing up. The one who played Barbies with me as kids because I promised him I'd do whatever he wanted if he'd just play Barbies with me first. My brother, the source of all my friends' first crushes growing up. He was gone. His body uninhabited.

Like the rings of a tree that tell the story of the years in which the tree lived, 2014 is one of the most significant rings in my life. We don't know when our time will come and it might never make sense. Too many of us live as if we have lots of life left. I pray that we do, but we might not. It wouldn't be healthy to live everyday like we were dying, but I do think it's healthier to make decisions knowing we might not have a lifetime ahead of us, that our purpose should be considered today, not ten years from now. You'll never have the clear path or all tools for the journey; the tools are what you acquire along the journey.

I can't say that I don't take anything for granted anymore—that just wouldn't be realistic. But I do have a different outlook on time now. As morbid as it might sound, the vantage point I use to evaluate all my high-level decisions is from my deathbed. What would I have wanted the story to look like when I'm at the end of my life, or if my life were suddenly taken from me? This question helps get me out of the present realities and all the fears that come with any risk and contemplate what truly maters. A lifetime can feel like, well, like a lifetime, but when you really stop to think about our time on this planet, we're here for a moment in time. It's up to each and every one of us to make the most of our time here.

Becoming the Entrepreneur of Your Life – YOU!

In the book *The 4-Hour Workweek* by Timothy Ferriss, he introduces the concept of lifestyle design. Ferriss argues that we should reconsider the old concepts of retirement and deferred life planning. That living today and engineering your life for maximum benefit now instead of post-retirement is the new goal. My belief is that in order to design your best life, you're going to need to think like an entrepreneur, a balanced one. There will be risk involved, but the return will far outweigh the cost.

It is my honor and privilege to be sharing my story with you through this book, what I've learned along the way, and why you absolutely can "have it all." In the perfect world, we would be doing this over a bottle of wine. Pouring out our dreams and struggles to one another as we pour each of us a glass. Yes, there would be more than one glass, because having one glass of wine is like eating only one Oreo and because we have lots to discuss. We've got one shot at this beautiful gift called life and it's relatively short. The entrepreneur of your life is you! You get to choose how you spend your time here, who you spend your time with, and the impact you will have on those around you.

I'm not going to tell you it's easy, but it's totally worth it. I had no idea my journey would lead me to where I'm sitting today, as a serial entrepreneur and mom. But balanced entrepreneurship is what taught me how to run my life for the best outcome today and for future years. I want to give this gift to you and I pray you take it up. Your best life is waiting and the only person who can create that life is YOU!

CHAPTER 1

What Makes an Entrepreneur?

"If you can see your path laid out in front of you step by step, you know it's not your path. Your own path you make with every step you take. That's why it's your path."

—Joseph Campbell

WHAT MAKES AN entrepreneur? Can anyone be an entrepreneur? How soon after one starts or purchases a business are they considered an entrepreneur? These are some of the questions I grappled with when I started my first company. But one thing stands out as my first major hurdle on my path to becoming an entrepreneur: my own biases.

I had to overcome my own unconscious beliefs about women and entrepreneurship. When I thought of an entrepreneur, the first image to come to mind was certainly not a woman, let alone a twenty-something, or a mother. In my mind, entrepreneurship was for men, not women, and the bar was high. Because of these biases, I didn't immediately embrace my journey. It wasn't until I had sold my first business and started a couple of others that I was finally able to accept and take pride in who I was as an entrepreneur. Why couldn't I step out proudly and claim my role as a strong female entrepreneur when I was twenty-five years old and starting my first company? The answer is complex, but it is also based on a broader, unconscious societal belief.

Halla Tómasdóttier, an Icelandic entrepreneur and former presidential candidate, illustrated this unconscious bias in action in an NPR podcast titled "How Can Leaders Inspire Others to Lead" (May 18, 2018). Halla did a volunteer teaching stint at her daughter's school and asked all of the thirteen-year-old boys and girls to draw some pictures. She was coming in to talk about career choices, so she asked them to draw pictures of a president, an entrepreneur, and a teacher—all three things she had achieved or worked towards herself. She did this exercise with many, many classes. All of the kids, with the exception of two, drew a male president, a male entrepreneur, and a female teacher. Keep in mind that Halla did this experiment in Iceland, a country that's generally considered to be leading the world when it comes to closing the gender gap. When asked to draw a leader, almost all of the students thought of a man. This visual is not far off from how many of us envision certain roles. When we think of a stereotypical entrepreneur, a woman is probably not the first to come to mind, let alone a mom with a child on her hip.

How we think about entrepreneurship matters because, on our subconscious and conscious levels, we are deciding whether or not we support those who step out of stereotypical roles and whether we will consider stepping out ourselves. When I started my first business, I was twenty-five years old and I couldn't bring myself to own the title of entrepreneur. Not yet.

The Recession

It was during the Recession of 2008. As an inexperienced advertising account executive, I had absolutely no idea what I was doing, so there weren't exactly people lined up to hire me. Thanks to the struggling economy, I decided I needed to create my own job. Therefore, my first business venture came more out of necessity than some well-thought-out grand vision. Sitting in what was normally an intimidating conference room, I felt calm. Even a little excited. Today, the team wasn't pitching a client on a new marketing campaign or the next catchy commercial. We were waiting for the arrival of our president to kick off this month's staff meeting. I sat in my seat at the conference table, enjoying the treats I had brought in that month: croissants, fresh fruit, and cheese. As I took a bite of the buttery croissant, my face warmed by the winter sun spilling through the expansive window overlooking downtown, I couldn't help but feel hopeful. I believed things were finally going to turn around after months of some of the worst financial drops in the history of the company. Month after month, at the regularly scheduled monthly staff meeting, our president would share the company financials. And every month, as we anxiously awaited better news than the month before, we would be surprised by the persistent decline. Up to that point, we had managed through the downturn, but everyone sitting in the conference room that day knew we couldn't continue operating if the financials continued to fall at an ever-increasing rate. Despite those fears, I clung to the hope that the recession would end soon and things would go back to the way they had been before.

We weren't the only ones experiencing this economic downturn. In early 2008, by anyone's account, the economy was in the tank and getting worse by the day. No one was safe.

We were smack dab in the middle of the worst global recession since the Great Depression in the 1930s. It had been about six months and everyone hoped the worst was past us, that things were going to turn around, and that numbers would start to climb again, but that was wishful thinking.

As our president walked into the room, any hope of good news quickly went out the sunny window. The expression on his face and the way he hurriedly entered the room, without engaging in his usual interoffice banter, gave us all we needed to know. He delivered the news we all had feared: we had experienced another record-breaking low month. We all looked to him for answers, but with a sullen expression of surrender, he said that things would be changing, that the recession was too much for our small company to bear, and that we would all need to carry the financial strain. Effective immediately, we would receive a significant reduction in our pay.

As he delivered the news, I heard a gasp from behind me. When I turned to look, I saw it was coming from one of my coworkers, Nikki. Tears were beginning to form in her eyes and her hand was covering her mouth, which lay open in shock. Nikki was the primary income earner in her family and things had already gotten too tight at home for her small family. She clearly didn't know how they would make ends meet with this new cut. She wasn't the only one whose head was reeling from the news. We would all try to make sense of the situation and the new reality, finding our own ways to cope and in our own time.

We went through another round of pay cuts and eventually the layoffs started. What had once been a fun work environment had changed to one that felt like dog eat dog. Fearful of losing their jobs, people started protecting their workloads in hopes of appearing valuable and irreplaceable. We worked more and were paid significantly less. The fun was gone, and going into work felt like work, like a job.

My Mental Shift

It was during this time that a major mental shift took place for me that would change the direction of my career. Up until that point, I had enjoyed my career and the places I'd worked. I never questioned traditional employment or considered entrepreneurship because I was just starting out and wanted to learn all that I could in my field in order to be a valuable employee. I enjoyed working. Work gave me purpose. I was proud of what I was learning and who I was becoming. Going into the office was an exciting adventure. My coworkers became my new friends, and I learned all about their lives over lunches out and the occasional happy hours downtown. I was young, and I loved learning what it was like to make friends with people ten, even twenty years my senior. I had no reason to believe this wouldn't always be the case. It was what I thought having a fulfilling career meant and I loved every part of it.

After a particularly long client meeting one afternoon, driving back to the office, my colleague Beth turned to me and said, "I don't know if I can take much more. My husband never wanted me to take this job in the first place. I know he needs my help at home with the kids and on the farm, but I wanted this for me. I wanted something for myself, a job that I was excited about; but now I just don't know if it's worth it. It's getting harder and harder to justify paying for childcare when my salary keeps getting cut."

I nodded my head in understanding as she spoke. This wasn't the first time I'd discussed the cost-of-working-versus-staying-home dilemma with someone; it had been happening a lot lately.

That's how the recession changed many workers' mindsets about work; instead of looking towards the future and imagining what was possible, many people had focused on their present reality. Everyone was concerned with how to get by on less, because people's time was worth less. In the case of my coworker Beth, it made more sense to give up her salary to help out at home. She was giving in, or at least that's how it seemed to me at the time.

I didn't understand how, through the course of only a few months and a handful of pay cuts, everyone around me had lost hope. I wanted to fight and I wanted others to step up with me. I believed we needed to be more creative, look for solutions, and step outside of our comfort zones. The dire reality we were in didn't scare me; it made me hungrier. I felt more driven than ever. It was during this time that I realized I loved working so much that I would have done it for free so long as it was purposeful and fulfilling. I simply could not understand why so many people were throwing in the towel.

That day in the car, as Beth confessed she was going to leave and stay at home, something inside of me snapped. I couldn't take another person giving in and leaving. I knew she had to do what was right for her family, but I struggled with her decision and couldn't understand why she and others were walking away. We were all feeling the economic pinch, but it was the people giving up that affected me the most.

Sitting in the car, I decided I would work for myself and I announced it to my colleague right there in the car. I have no clue where that idea came from, and even as the words were tumbling from my mouth, I didn't believe what I was saying. It was not a conscious decision or a path I had been considering prior to that day, but once it came out, I couldn't ignore it.

On March 8, 2008 in Wisconsin, with snow falling all around us, my husband and I were married. I didn't know it at the time of our wedding, but just two months later my entrepreneurial vision would become a reality.

The Leap

Sarah had been my boss and the one responsible for letting people go as our company struggled through the recession. She was a savvy public relations maven who had moved to our small community from California. She was worldly and understood more about communications than anyone in our area. The work she did was the reason the company was still standing through the tough times. She was ten years older than me and lightyears ahead in business acumen. Everything from the clothes she wore to the way she carried herself and how she commanded the presence of the room intrigued me. I found her personality and aura infectious.

We had grown closer through the downturn because the recession had lit a flame under both of us. We were both passionate about our work and saw an opportunity that had been created as a result of the struggling economy. During one of our office chats, we dreamed out loud about starting a business together. And that's exactly what we did.

At the time, I didn't understand why Sarah chose to start a public relations business with me. I didn't feel as though I brought much to the table. I was relatively inexperienced and didn't know a thing about public relations. But I was hungry. The recession had created a resolve and a hunger in me to figure it out. I didn't want to give up like others, or go to a job that sucked the life out of me, so I would start my own business. We began dreaming up plans for a public relations company that helped companies with communications and social media.

Sarah often wore a pair of red shoes to work, an act of

defiance to what was happening around us. It was those shoes that would inspire me to name our company. We drew up our logo on a napkin in a coffee shop and sent it to a designer. We were careful to keep everything quiet during the two months we were creating our plans because we were creating direct competition for our current employer. It was an exciting time but also extremely stressful. My stomach was constantly in knots and I rarely got a good night's sleep as my wheels were turning with new ideas and a renewed excitement. We wrote the business plan in a week and hired an attorney to file our business entity and draft the legal documents. Despite how quickly it happened, we wanted to get it right because these would serve as the foundation of the company.

Walking into the legal office building, I was intimidated and full of nervous excitement. This was real; it was happening; we were starting a business. The lady at the front desk asked our names and led us to a small conference room with book-lined shelves. I recognized the books as the wall that served as the backdrop for all their cheesy headshots on the website and marketing materials.

As the attorney walked in the room, I noticed that he was shorter than I expected and looked angry from years of arguing and fighting. We had hired him because we heard he was a "bulldog" and apparently when it comes to attorneys that's what you want. He recommended that we file our organization as an S-Corp and asked how we'd like to divide the ownership. We hadn't thought about the ownership structure up to that point.

I turned to Sarah, looking to her for answers, as I often did during that time. She looked at the attorney and said, "Well, we can't be 50/50 right? People don't recommend that, do they?"

The attorney answered her matter-of-factly, "No, that's never a good idea. When you're 50/50, you both have an equal say in decisions and no one can trump the other. You'll want one of you to have the final say when things get tough."

Nodding her head, Sarah turned to me, gauging my reaction. I didn't like how he said we couldn't have equal say. We'd had equal say up to that point and it was working well for us, but I knew Sarah well enough to know she would follow the attorney's advice. She was very concerned about making any missteps, so if the attorney was recommending anything other than 50/50, she was going to do what he said.

I looked at her and said, "You should probably be the majority, right?" I was afraid of being cut out of the deal. I was well aware of the fact that I didn't bring a whole lot of knowledge or experience to the table, so I folded first. I figured any part of the deal is better than nothing and 49 is almost 50.

She shrugged her shoulders and gave a little laugh at the simplicity of it all and said, "Sure, sounds good to me!"

As we left the office that day, we decided to grab a beer at the restaurant near the attorney's office. We wanted to remember this moment and celebrate. The paperwork was filed and we were officially in business. We had brought our business plan to multiple banks hoping for a loan to get started but, in 2008, getting a business loan was nearly impossible for a startup. So we were forced to take out a business credit card and finance what we could on the card. We hated that this was the only option, but it forced us to spend as little as possible and pay off the debt as quickly as money came in. We opened a 400 square-foot office space by May 2008. That's how it went. We made decisions quickly and forged ahead fast.

Our first year in business felt like a blur. We were flying high on our adrenaline and dreams. On the outside, we appeared confident and self-assured. People asked all the time if we were scared about going out on our own, but we were moving too fast to be scared. There was no time for fear once we started. We had made the decision and had no choice but to pour everything into the business. We were fortunate—the business soared despite the tough economic times because we identified how we could serve local businesses. We offered new solutions to the challenges companies were facing.

The business was making waves in our small community and it wasn't long before some of the largest companies in our local area hired us. We were making a name for ourselves and from the outside looking in, everything seemed to be going better than expected. But the real struggle wasn't how the business was doing and whether or not we were making money. The real struggle was my internal experience. I struggled with how I viewed myself and who I was. I didn't feel like an entrepreneur because I didn't fit the stereotypical mold and felt as though I had to prove that I was worthy. And my lack of identity made it hard to feel valuable.

If you would have asked me prior to 2008 if entrepreneurs are born or made, I would have told you I believe some of us are just meant to be entrepreneurs, that we are born. After my experience with the recession and all that followed, I realized then and now firmly believe that entrepreneurs are made. Circumstances and environment play critical roles in our lives and drive many decisions and outcomes. The fact that the economy was incredibly strained early on changed the entire trajectory of my career. I had no idea that I would become an entrepreneur, but that's how it played out.

Over the years, my own internal definition of entrepreneurship has changed significantly. And similarly, when I ask others what makes an entrepreneur, I receive all sorts of answers. Their answers have to do with their background, their opinions, or because they know people who have owned businesses. The interesting thing is that the more you dig in, the more you realize that the definition is all over the board and varies depending on who you ask.

What is an Entrepreneur Anyway?

After starting the public relations firm, people began referring to me as an "entrepreneur." Part of me really wanted that to be true but as I mentioned, inside I felt like a fraud by accepting that title before proving myself. It wasn't because I didn't want to be known as an entrepreneur, quite the opposite actually. I just didn't believe I had earned that title yet. In my mind, people earned it by successfully founding or purchasing businesses, not through simply starting a yet-to-be-determined-successful business. In my mind, it wasn't a position you stumbled upon by starting one company; rather, it was a title you earned through hard work and running at least one successful business.

Like many people, the image in my mind of what I considered the "ideal entrepreneur" was a powerful person, typically male, always put together and powerful. This person exuded confidence and commanded the presence of a room. They didn't second guess their decisions because they had a confidence in themselves and their abilities that most of us can only begin to imagine. They made good decisions quickly and people followed their leadership. I imagined that they came from a good, name-brand school and grew up in a part of the country that was much more intimidating than my home state of Wisconsin. This person, the entrepreneur, was everything I wasn't. If I had kept this stereotypical definition, I would have never amounted to the ideal of this entrepreneur and very few people in my network would have, either.

The way I was defining entrepreneur wasn't based in reality or what actually makes someone an entrepreneur. I was thinking mostly of someone's background, how they looked, and their personality traits. While those things can be helpful, they aren't what actually defines an entrepreneur. The truth is that my definition was naïve and extremely limited. I wasn't remembering that any time you start something new and stretch yourself, you're not going to be good at it. Think about the title "author." You can't tell me that everyone who writes their first book owns that title immediately. For many people, it takes time and through the process, the title grows on them. It's like trying on high heels as a child. They don't fit; your toes are crammed into the front, and your heels end far short of where they should. When you walk, they drag across the floor, and even though they look ridiculous, they make you feel fabulous. This is the attitude to take when growing into any new and uncomfortable role. You won't feel like you fit the definition and you might not even look the part, but that doesn't make you any less worthy. When we're learning something new, we're not good at it immediately. The learning process is messy and full of failure, but that's how we learn! When I first started out, I wasn't being patient with myself and my journey.

Why does it matter how we define and imagine entrepreneurs? Since starting the public relations firm, I have gone on to meet and work with hundreds of entrepreneurs. I can't think of a single one that matched my previous narrow definition. Just like the example from the children in Iceland who imagined a female teacher but a male entrepreneur and president, many of us carry unconscious biases. If this is our internal definition, how many women will imagine themselves in these roles? Perhaps fewer women brave entrepreneurship because we think we don't look the part. It's time to reimagine the role of the entrepreneur and create a different reality.

Part of why it's tricky to fully understand what makes an entrepreneur is the fact that it's not cut and dry. There are online classes that teach entrepreneurship and at many schools and universities, you can now walk away with a degree in entrepreneurship, but is that what makes an entrepreneur? A certification or degree? Unlike a doctor, teacher, engineer, accountant, or nurse, entrepreneurship is a title that you earn through doing. If someone graduated with a degree in entrepreneurship and referred to themselves as an entrepreneur, people would naturally ask what businesses they've started or currently own. This is not the case with the other professions— when you graduate with any of those degrees, it becomes part of your identity.

The Actual Definition, Not What I Thought Made an Entrepreneur

It's important that we have a clear understanding of the true definition of an entrepreneur before we dive deeper into the idea of entrepreneurship. Let's start with the definition from Merriam-Webster, which says an entrepreneur is "one who organizes, manages, and assumes the risks of a business or enterprise" or "a person who starts a business and is willing to risk loss in order to make money." Notice that nowhere does the definition say anything about gender, how one looks, or whether the individual is an introvert or an extrovert. What it does say, however, is that an entrepreneur is a person who takes a risk on a business to make money. I want to break down this definition because I think many of us, myself included, don't fully consider all of these parts when defining entrepreneurship, or we get the parts twisted in our own definition.

1. A Person

The very first part of the definition defines **who** can be an entrepreneur. An entrepreneur is defined as a person and a person can be any gender. I know it seems silly to state the obvious, but the obvious isn't always so obvious. The children who drew an entrepreneur for Halla picked their images up from somewhere. And just as kids do, they stated what many of us believe or know but don't say—that entrepreneurship is a predominantly male role. This makes sense when you think back to my own internal definition and the characteristics I was assigning to an entrepreneur: power, leader, charisma, confident, and decisive. Women can certainly have and do have these characteristics, but they tend to be considered more masculine characteristics. The other important thing to recognize is that a person of any age can be an entrepreneur. The definition doesn't include specific backgrounds, professions, race, sexual preference or identity, disabilities or abilities, genealogy, personality traits, geographic areas, and so on. I think you get the point, but the point also has to be clearly stated. Perceptions become reality when we don't challenge them.

2. A Business

Now that we know Who, let's define What. To be an entrepreneur, this person must organize, manage, start, or assume the risk of a business or enterprise. But what makes a business? Again, we're going to lean on Merriam-Webster for this one so that there isn't any confusion. A business is "the activity of making, buying, or selling goods or providing services in exchange for money." Simply put, the purpose of a business is to make money through the exchange of goods or services. If we remove money from the definition, the purpose of a business would be to provide value so that there is an exchange of some sort. The exchange could be a barter or trade, depending on currency, but for our purposes and the purposes of this book, we'll stick to the currency of money. Our hypothetical person, to be considered an entrepreneur, must be responsible for a business for the purpose of making money. Are we all on the same page? Stay with me, I promise this is important.

3. Risk

The third part of the definition is that there must be risk involved. The definition doesn't say what kind of risk and this is where I've experienced the greatest confusion in the entrepreneurial community. Somehow, somewhere, someone decided that risk, when starting a business, must be financial. The only piece of the definition that specifically addresses money is in the making of money, not the investing of money. The truth is, risk can take many different forms, such as reputation, time, relationships, network, capital, or income. There is often also a financial investment in business, but not always and it's not required. Who knows, maybe back in the day you would give up one of your children in exchange for a business. I have no idea, but it might have happened! Regardless, it's time we eliminate this piece of the definition from our mindset. I would argue that there are things far more valuable than money such as time, reputation, and maybe even your children as a means of payment. As we're all well aware, time is limited, and I would argue it is the most valuable asset any one of us has. It cannot be purchased or sold; we can't make more of it, and none of us owns it. We can't say the same of money.

4. Return

The last piece of the puzzle is return. A person, to be considered an entrepreneur, has risked something to be responsible for a business for the purpose of making money. Again, if this book were written back in the day that we exchanged children for business, if that actually happened, the return might be measured by something other than money. But for our purposes, money is the currency. What I like about this end result is that it's black and white, quantifiable. A business must make money to be considered a business, and the person who has responsibility for that business would therefore be considered an entrepreneur.

This all seems pretty logical and straightforward, right? Well, unfortunately it's not. People come with their own thoughts and experiences around entrepreneurship and the waters can get a little muddy. For example, this idea of "ownership" when it comes to business is a sticky issue. Most people believe you need to "own" a business to be considered an entrepreneur. But take a look back at the definition—nowhere does it mention the word ownership. The assumption is that an entrepreneur owns their own business, but what exactly does ownership mean? In a traditional bricks and mortar business, if the business has a loan from the bank for the assets, who owns the business? If a franchisee opens a location leveraging a larger brand and organization, who owns that organization? What if the business took on capital investment and there are investors or shareholders involved? Do you see where this gets tough to nail down? Ownership means different things to different people and one person's definition of ownership might be entirely different than another's. While I do agree that an entrepreneur assumes responsibility for a business, and many times we refer to this as "ownership," it's important to know that the definition of ownership is also not the same across the board.

The very last point of disagreement I come across regularly is around investment and return. Again, the only part of the definition that specifically addresses money is in the making of money, not the investment of money. And in the making of money, the definition does not include an amount or percentage. The only requirement in the definition is that part of the purpose of the business or venture is to make money. Is a business that breaks even, covers costs, or reinvests back into the business less of a business? Absolutely not. And I would argue a nonprofit organization is no less a business, and the founders are no less entrepreneurs than a traditional for-profit business, even though their tax status is regulated by the nature of their entity. I know this is getting into the weeds, but it's important because all of the misperceptions and entrepreneur shaming I have heard and experienced are founded in not fully understanding these basic principles.

Entrepreneur Shaming and Giving Birth

If you and I were sitting with one another at a coffee shop, talking about entrepreneurship and what makes an entrepreneur, I would be passionately gesticulating with my hands so that you would understand how serious I am about this idea. I've experienced too much "entrepreneur shaming" out there and it needs to stop! Do you know where the entrepreneur shaming comes from? Other entrepreneurs! We all carry around different definitions and those of us who've started or purchased businesses seem to come with the biggest chip on our shoulders. Look, I get it; it's hard. This is not a career for the faint of heart and we all have battle wounds. We know all too well the reality of growing a business and we're not shy about sharing what we've accomplished. We talk about our wounds like mothers who've given birth. Unfortunately, this does very little for the person who's seeking advice except to totally freak them out! We have to understand that our advice can sometimes do more harm than good for those facing a similar path, just like birth stories. Each story is unique, messy, and beautiful, but in the end, it's your story and no one will have the same experience.

The same holds true for what it took each of us to grow in our entrepreneurial experiences. For some, it took a significant amount of capital and financial risk to start a business. For others, it took less capital but a whole host of risk in the form of reputation, network, or time. A significant capital investment doesn't always equal a significant return and vice versa. We need to stop assigning dollars to how entrepreneurial we think someone is. Money has very little to do with what it takes to be an entrepreneur. This is especially true in the beginning, when you're just getting started. Many novice entrepreneurs don't have a significant amount of money to invest in a business. But what they do have matters and it's valuable to them. If someone risks an investment of $1,000 in a business and someone else invests $100,000 in their venture, is the $100,000 person a riskier entrepreneur? It totally depends. What if the $1,000 entrepreneur has very little capital to invest and took a loan from a family member to start their business, while the $100,000 entrepreneur is a millionaire, and this is part of their growth strategy? We can never fully know the complete story and it's time we stop measuring (ahem…judging) others on their "entrepreneurness" solely based on investment and return.

The Business Baby and an Actual Baby

When we started our PR firm in May 2008, that business was my only birth story. By October of that year, the business was growing quickly, and we were enjoying our relatively fast success. We had hired our second employee, which brought our small team up to a total of four. Around that time, we were in the middle of securing our largest client and the second-largest employer in the region. We had endless meetings with high-level executives to explore how we could work together and how our team could support the overall organization. It was an exciting but nerve-wracking time, which left me feeling out of sorts. I felt sick to my stomach every day and even dizzy as I sat through long meetings negotiating contracts while checking the clock to see when I could use the bathroom next. One evening, while trying to balance during a yoga class and growing more and more frustrated by the dizziness I was experiencing, I decided to purchase a pregnancy test on the way home. I didn't actually think I was pregnant, but I wanted to rule out the possibility. I just figured I was feeling the effects of stress as the business was growing and the symptoms would subside with time.

When I arrived home that evening, my husband and I enjoyed dinner together. When we were done, I went upstairs to shower and get ready for bed. I never mentioned the pregnancy test because I figured it was no big deal and there was no sense in having an unnecessary discussion. After turning on the water for the shower, I took the test with little thought of the potential results. But when those two blue parallel lines showed up, confirming that I was pregnant, I fell to the floor. I yelled to my husband, who came running.

He stared at me from the doorway, trying to make sense of what was happening. I could see from the fear in his eyes that he thought something terrible had occurred. I was sobbing as I looked up and handed him the stick with the two blue lines. Even then it didn't register until I said, "I'm pregnant." As I said the words out loud, they let loose a whole new gush of tears from me. I'm embarrassed to admit that I wasn't immediately excited about being pregnant. I was terrified. My entire world and future shifted in an instant and I was in complete shock. I thought of my business and our easy, carefree life. It was gone. A baby is a big deal. A baby is forever.

I watched the rush of relief pass through his face as he let out the breath he had been holding. Tears came to his eyes too but his were different. His tears were happy, and a smile spread across his face. He didn't say anything as he slid to the floor and took my trembling body into his arms. We sat there for a long time while we both cried for different reasons. Eventually we moved to the couch downstairs, where I stared at those two blue lines for hours in shock.

The business was my first baby, but I was pregnant with an actual baby just six months later. It was a God-given blessing, but it was a surprise and we weren't ready to become parents. We were still getting acclimated to a life in entrepreneurship and all the responsibilities that come with owning a business. Looking back now, I am confident that while this wasn't part of our plan, this was part of His plan. The entrepreneur I was before and after children is distinctly different. Like they say, nothing can prepare you for how children will change your life and because I had the business before the baby, I had to learn, through a lot of pain and tears, how to have both.

When my daughter Wren was born, I took six weeks off and did my best to work from home around feeding and naps. The business was about fifteen months old by that point and I didn't believe I could take excess time to be with her; just writing that sentence breaks my heart and still brings tears to my eyes. I am not someone who says they live without regrets; I have regrets and I have some from that phase in my life. As I said in the introduction, this is the book I wish I had available to me when I was young, starting a business, and becoming a mom. Wren went to daycare at six weeks old. I was doing the best I could to manage all that was on my plate. I was young, unsure of my decisions, and struggled to think long-term and what was best for the future. The truth was, I also really loved what I was doing with the business and even when I was home on maternity leave, I missed it. I felt a tremendous sense of responsibility for raising both my daughter and my business. Starting a family put very tangible value on my time. I became aware of how and where I spent my time. I did my best to be where my feet were. When I was at work, I tried to keep my thoughts focused on work. When I was at home, I tried to keep my thoughts off of business. That first year of my daughter's life felt like an exhausting train wreck. Wren was a colicky baby and we didn't get a full night of sleep until she was nine months old. I still remember driving to work one day and having absolutely no idea how I had gotten there after I had arrived. I was sleep deprived and stressed to the max with the business growth and being a new mom. The stress was too much to bear. After seeking help from my OB, I was diagnosed with postpartum depression and began taking an anti-depressant and anti-anxiety medication. I tried to maintain the façade of successful entrepreneur mom who had it all together, but the reality was quite different. I felt like a failure in business and a failure as mom. I knew I couldn't live that way for long.

Pursuing Balance

I never chose balance to be my "thing." It chose me. Every time someone said the word, my ears would perk up. I started listening to how people felt about the idea of balance. At first, I knew I needed to figure out how to succeed as a mom and an entrepreneur with balance, but it quickly grew into a curiosity and fascination about the polarization of the topic. Some believe you continually work towards balance every day, never fully achieving it but always striving. Others believe it's an impossible standard that people need to eliminate from their vocabularies because the simple pursuit of it makes people miserable. I certainly didn't agree that pursuing balance made people miserable, but I also didn't know where I stood exactly. I believed it was a necessity if you were going to have a family and successful career, but it also felt so much larger than just managing those two aspects of one's life. My curiosity and desire to figure out how to balance it all took me on a ten-year journey through multiple children and even more business ventures. It was this obsession with balance that was responsible for ending my first business partnership with Sarah when I sold my shares; I hadn't been finding the balance I needed with that company for the stage we were in as a family. I desired greater flexibility—to work from home and at varying times, depending on my daughter's needs. I knew family had to come before business, but because that business had come before the family, I wasn't capable of making a shift. Balance became a keystone in my career as an entrepreneur and with each new business venture, another piece of the puzzle fell into place. Eventually I had a clear roadmap for how to have it all and do it really well.

One Size Does Not Fit All in Entrepreneurship

Since starting my first business, I have gone on to start and purchase a handful of others. I've learned a lot about different types of businesses and the people who run them. I've discovered that entrepreneurship is less about what's on paper and more about mindset. Entrepreneurs can be found in all industries and all types of businesses. I've learned that what it takes to create a successful social commerce or direct sales business is exactly what it takes to create a successful bricks and mortar business. Neither is less than or more important than the other. This matters because people are different and their situations call for different solutions. I was able to start a public relations company at twenty-five years old and pour my life into that startup because it was just me and my husband running our small home. I worked early mornings, late nights, and every weekend because I didn't have children to care for yet. We were able to forgo my income because cutting back only affected the two of us.

If the situation had been different, if we had originally had children and relied on my income, I don't know if we could have taken the same risks on a bricks and mortar business. There's no way of knowing, but what I do know is that everyone's situation is unique and calls for distinct solutions. Each one of us has to choose what's best for our households without fear of judgment or criticism. As I sit here today, with two children under the age of ten, I run very different businesses. Our situation has changed and what works for our small family now is totally different than what worked ten years ago. My businesses are all virtual and I run them from home. I have partners instead of employees. My goal is to model for my girls that they can have it all through balance: the purposeful career and a deeply fulfilling life.

I want to inspire other women by telling my own story so that they too can have it all. We need women to buy into this belief because women bring different strengths to the table which are beneficial for the future of business and the next generation of leaders. What we can see, we can believe. And the more women we have in entrepreneurial positions, the more will be inspired to step up. Women tend to be the primary caregivers in the home, which is what holds many back from pursuing a career in entrepreneurship. Somewhere along the way we started believing we had to choose: We could have the family or we could have the career, but we couldn't have both. Having both meant one was suffering and in the worst cases, women were being judged and shamed for being "bad mothers" for wanting a career.

Entrepreneurship is the ultimate career expression because running your own business is a tremendous responsibility. Just like raising a child, a business takes time to grow, lots of attention and energy, and requires the heart of the one who's responsible. Women, by our very nature, are the only gender physically capable of growing another being inside ourselves. The heart and soul we were given to care for new life are tremendous gifts in business as well. We need more value-based leadership and women, when leading with our natural gifts, are natural-born entrepreneurs. That being said, a critical piece of the puzzle is balance. Because women typically wear many hats at home and at work, the only way we can be effective entrepreneurs is through the pursuit of balance. This is not simply work/life balance, however. This is a multi-faceted approach to balance that puts the entrepreneur at the center with her values around her, ensuring that each one is a priority, and that each is an important ingredient of her success pie.

Journaling Prompts: Putting Pen to Paper and Getting Real

1. I shared that my internal definition or entrepreneurship was holding me back from pursuing my purpose and owning my role as an entrepreneur. What is your definition of entrepreneur? Do you hold a similar erroneous definition? Take some time to journal about how you see entrepreneurs and those who start, purchase and build businesses.

2. The definition of entrepreneurship is "a person who starts a business and is willing to risk loss in order to make money." Out of the four key aspects: a person, a business, risk and return, which element(s) cause you to pause and question your ability to be an entrepreneur?

3. I was blessed, the recession created a hunger and resolve in me to figure it out and start a business. The biggest threat to pursuing our dreams is comfort and security. What dreams do you hold in your heart that you are not pursuing? What would you do if you knew you could not fail? Take time to journal about your dreams before proceeding to the next chapter.

Taking the Lesson One Step Further with Recommended Reading

The Crossroads of Should and Must – Find and Follow Your Passion, by Elle Luna

One Action Step to Build Momentum

Think of someone you know who's started her own business and reach out to her to ask her to coffee. Ask her how she started her business, where the idea came from, what fears almost stopped her and what's the best part about being an entrepreneur. Make sure to listen and ask good questions so that you can learn from her experience. The superheroes we hold in high regard are actually remarkably similar to us and when you understand that she was afraid too but took the next step, it will begin to build your confidence that you can as well.

CHAPTER 2

Tapping into Your Inner Self and Building an Army of Belief

"Our deepest fear is not that we are inadequate. Our deepest fear is that we are powerful beyond measure. It is our light, not our darkness that most frightens us. We ask ourselves, 'Who am I to be brilliant, gorgeous, talented, fabulous?' Actually, who are you not to be? You are a child of God. Your playing small does not serve the world. There is nothing enlightened about shrinking so that other people won't feel insecure around you. We are all meant to shine, as children do. We were born to make manifest the glory of God that is within us. It's not just in some of us; it's in everyone. And as we let our own light shine, we unconsciously give other people permission to do the same. As we are liberated from our own fear, our presence automatically liberates others."

—Marianne Williamson, *A Return to Love: Reflections on the Principles of "A Course in Miracles"*

What's on your business card?

OVING INTO THE 400 square-foot office space happened fast and furious because time was of the essence and we wanted to be up and running as quickly as possible. We hired painters to brighten up the colors of the walls while we set up the Ikea desks, chairs, and conference table. This was my first experience setting up an office and I wanted it to be bright, vibrant, and energetic so that we would be excited coming to work. I wanted it to be a reflection of the brand we were building and a place where we would enjoy spending time.

Setting up the office was surreal, much like buying your first home. No one was telling us when to come in or what to do; it was all up to us. The three of us—my business partner, our first employee, and I—spent the first few months on equal parts establishing the business and building the business. One moment we were meeting with potential clients, and the next we were interviewing vendors to create signage, a website, and various elements of a new business. Early on, we didn't have titles or job descriptions, so everyone pitched in where help was needed. It was fun! We were a team. Even though my partner and I owned the business, we didn't keep anything from our first and only employee. The three of us were in it together and we spent every minute of every day together for the first couple weeks.

During this time of getting our feet underneath us, we needed to create business cards. It was one of the easier tasks we had to complete, far easier than the website, the legal documents, or the employee binder. I thought all we needed on the cards was our logo, our names, and our contact information. I had forgotten that we'd also need titles, which are an important part of business cards. But we had never discussed titles. The three of us were a team; we did everything together. We didn't have titles because we hadn't needed them.

When we were designing our business cards, Sarah, my business partner, turned to me and asked, "What do you want your title to be on your card?" It was a simple enough question, but I was completely stumped. No one had ever asked me what title I *wanted*. Titles were typically assigned, something someone else gave to you; they came with job descriptions and responsibilities. Titles carried significance and meaning because they immediately informed others who you were within a company. I'd only had a few titles up to that point, so I answered with what came naturally, what was comfortable.

"I'll be an account executive," I said. Even as I said it, I could sense that Sarah didn't think this was the right answer by the long pause and look of confusion and amusement on her face.

She laughed, "You can't be an account executive; you own half of the company!"

I don't remember any discussion after that point; she just put me down as "Vice President."

I still remember looking at my business card for the first time. It was stark white with a bright red, powerful shoe on the front. The cardstock was thick; it implied we were serious, we meant business. It was clean and crisp, and portrayed the professionalism we were after. Then I remember seeing my name and "Vice President" immediately below it. It felt like I was looking at a different Jessica Dennis' card. My title was the largest, most intimidating pair of red shoes and they didn't fit. Not yet.

Every time I handed my card to a potential client or spoke my title out loud, I felt like an impostor. When having to introduce myself, I would say my title more as a question than a statement, waiting for someone to answer with, "Oh no, you're not." Even though I had started this business, I still felt like the account executive from my previous role. I didn't feel like a business owner or an entrepreneur, let alone a vice president! This was stretching me way outside of my comfort zone; the Jessica Dennis on the card and the Jessica Dennis I felt like were an ocean apart. I didn't know how to become that future self, and at times it felt like I'd never be her.

What I learned from that experience is that a title is just a title. We're the ones who assign all of the meaning to it—whether it's more or less important than others and whether or not we measure up. My reaction to being labeled a Vice President was similar to being called an entrepreneur; I wanted to do the work to know I was capable before I took on the identity. Women tend to react this way more than men. Men will go for a position that's outside of their experience, knowing that if they land the position, they'll figure it out later. Women, on the other hand, like to know they'll be qualified before they put themselves out there and speak up.

In the book *Secrets of Six-Figure Women* by Barbara Stanny, she addresses this very idea and why women are passed up for positions that they're qualified for. Stanny argues that the reason women don't put themselves out there more is simply a matter of recognizing our worth. "Underlying our unwillingness to speak up is a woman's own inclination to devalue herself . . . . When you have a sense of your worth, higher salaries seem to follow suit, simply because you're more inclined to make sure they do" (pg. 155).

It comes down to our belief and confidence in our abilities, which are critically important for entrepreneurship. The good news is that we don't have to be born with an unlimited supply of confidence, we can actually develop it. But to do that, we need to stretch ourselves and dare to reach for more.

Is There More to it Than Just Believing in Myself?

For the rest of this chapter, we're going to walk through different internal and external forces that are available to us that we can tap into in order to build belief in ourselves. Belief and tapping into oneself is critical because there will be all sorts of outside pressures around you. Pressures to do certain things or be certain people based on what's needed but knowing who you are and listening to your inner voice will give you the confidence to walk your own path. Walking your path is what will allow you to build balance. The whole concept of believing in oneself seems complicated at the outset because it's more of a feeling than logic or reason, and there are also varying degrees of belief that can ebb and flow at different points in our lives. We may walk through a few years where we felt unstoppable and limitless, only to be followed by a period of doubt and insecurity. All of this is completely normal.

I am going to refer to gut instinct, confidence, inner voice, and external forces or a higher power. They're all just slightly different and it makes sense to describe them here so that you don't get tripped up as you read on. We will start with gut instinct, which is something you feel specifically when it comes to making decisions, trusting that your body knows the best route for you in a particular decision. Confidence is a belief in oneself that you are capable, built through action and over time, not static, but ever-changing. Your inner voice is similar to gut instinct but is more specifically thoughts or nudges pulling you in the direction of your purpose or the greatness we referred to at the beginning of this book. This inner voice is not necessarily a guide for decision making like gut instinct is; it's in play all the time trying to lead you in a specific direction. Lastly, we will discuss external forces or a higher power. These forces are highly dependent on your belief system and are different for everyone. For some, it's The Universe and the natural forces around all of us. For others, it's God and His direction for your life. These external forces are things that happen to us and for us that are pushing us in an intended, purposeful direction.

Building Belief and Instincts

"Fake it till you make it."

That's the advice I received most often when I was feeling less than confident in my new role as an entrepreneur. The sentiment behind the statement makes sense: Put one foot in front of the other, act as if you fit the role and know what you're doing until you actually know what you're doing. But to me the statement also felt cheesy and dishonest. I've heard people say it other ways too: "Preach it till you believe it" and "Faith it till you make it." Out of all of them, I prefer, "Faith it till you make it" because there's nothing dishonest about it. It takes belief and faith in yourself, your situation, and forces outside of your control to pursue your purpose.

One thing all entrepreneurs need in spades is belief. They need a belief in themselves but also in their circumstances, timing, and even a higher purpose. When I started the PR firm, I was surprised by how many professionals referred to my "gut" when making decisions. They were interested in the numbers and logic and reason, but many times they would ask what my gut was telling me. We all have it—our gut instinct and intuition. The gut instinct is something you feel more than something you consciously understand on an intellectual level. It's that feeling when something just feels "off" or when something feels right, regardless of what it looks like on paper or what our brains tell us. For the entrepreneur, learning to listen to this inner guide and allow decisions to be made from a place of feeling as well as logic and reason is a powerful tool. The thing about belief and listening to your intuition is that it's not black and white. No one else can feel it but you. When I look back at my entry into entrepreneurship and all the questions I had about what makes an entrepreneur, it came down to my belief in myself. When you're an employee, you're hired to perform a job with specific responsibilities, and you're paid to do it. As an entrepreneur, you're the boss and you have to believe in yourself. People can give you advice and you can (and should) read all sorts of books, but at the end of the day, you're the one calling the shots. This is not a soft, "I think I can, I think I can" kind of belief. This is the kind of belief that creates a determination deep down inside, a fire in your belly. It's a resolve to figure it out when you don't know how and pick yourself up and try again when you fail. You might not even know you have this strength until you find yourself in situations in which you need it, but the good news is, it can be developed. I believe all of us were created with it, even if we can't feel it. You only need a tiny piece of this belief to get started and then it can be developed from there.

You Gotta Believe in YOU!

Confidence in yourself is the foundation of taking risks, and risk is an essential part of being an entrepreneur, remember? If you don't believe in yourself, you're probably not going to risk what's comfortable. Confidence is simply belief in yourself and your ability to succeed. It is not a static measurement, however; our confidence can rise or fall depending on situations and moments in time. Imagine something you're good at, maybe it's writing or playing an instrument. Your confidence as it relates to those activities is high because you know you're capable. That same confidence might not show up if you try something new, like Brazilian jujitsu or rock climbing. Think about measuring confidence on a sliding scale. The task is the slider and has the ability to move. In this example, you can also think of confidence as skillset or competency. On each end of the scale are opposing values, one end is marked "low proficiency or beginner" and the other is "proficient or expert." The slider can move from one end to the other and as it moves, it measures skillset, which increases as it moves closer to the end marked proficient. If your confidence slider is closer to the end marked beginner, your skillset is low and your confidence is low. The closer the slider moves to the other end, the more your skillset increases, therefore your confidence grows. Confidence is not a static measurement, it is constantly changing in different situations and at different points in time.

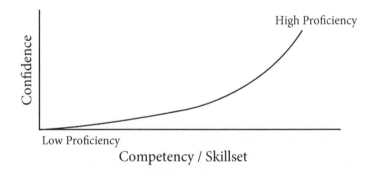

For example, consider someone who is learning to play basketball. Basketball is the activity or task and your confidence will grow as you improve your skills. If you keep doing this in different activities, your confidence in yourself and your belief that you can develop new skillsets will increase. When I started my first company, my confidence was low because I had never started a company before, but I had pushed myself up to that point and knew that when I applied myself, I could learn new skills. You can develop and strengthen your confidence by trying new things and learning new skills. And you can then transfer the confidence you develop to other activities. This sliver of belief in yourself is absolutely necessary for trying new things. We're creatures of comfort and our primal brains do not like doing things that put us in danger. Starting a business and putting ourselves out there is a risk and it's scary. There's no way of knowing when you start how everything will play out, but if you believe in yourself and you have confidence in your ability to learn new skills, a sliver is all it takes to get started.

Listening to Your Inner Voice

Have you ever heard your inner voice? We have all sorts of thoughts throughout the day, but they don't all carry the same weight, and they shouldn't. We all have a guide within us, our inner voice that is leading us in the right direction. My inner voice reveals itself as a thought that crosses my mind and stands out more than others, stirring something inside of me. That day in the car with my colleague, when I said I would own my own business—that was my inner voice. This experience has happened a few times throughout my life and I've learned to listen because they come from my truest self. Deeper than your gut instinct, these nudges come from the deepest, most authentic part of ourselves.

That day in the car, the idea of working for myself was one of the first times I'd felt this nudge. In the moment, I remember looking to my friend and measuring her reaction because I had no idea where it had come from or if I was actually capable of owning a business. And if I was capable of owning a business,

I had no idea when or how that could happen. I figured I'd see suspicion all over her face.

Instead, she had very little reaction at all. Looking back, I realize that people respond to how we say things more than what we say. If you're going to say something crazy like, "I'm going to start my own business," and say it as a statement with confidence, people will likely believe you. The way we think internally and speak externally also has a profound impact on what our subconscious believes. Sometimes we need to trick ourselves into believing the crazy things we think and say just as we would need to convince others. The words might come tumbling out or the thought crosses your mind and the first time you speak it out loud, you might feel like an impostor. You might feel like a fake. The next voice you hear might say, "You're not an entrepreneur. You can't run your own business." At least that's what my brain told me immediately after I admitted this little entrepreneurial dream, but when you know that voice is coming, you can also choose not to listen to it.

All of my internal nudges have happened like that. Other examples include my million-dollar dream by thirty years old and writing this book you have in front of you. All of these callings have come as a singular idea at a very specific moment in time. They didn't come when I was ready for them, and in most cases I rejected them at first. But they persisted. The best way I can describe it is that it's an idea you can't shake and once you're aware of it, you'll notice all sorts of coincidences that happen around you.

Following a Higher Power

I want to share more with you about why I've come to listen to these nudges because they've made all the difference in my career and in my life. I've learned to follow them even though they bring up a whole host of fears and self-doubt. I believe they come from within us and apart from us. For me, they come from God Himself. They come from the one who made me and lives within me. For you, it might be different. You might not believe in God, and if that's the case, lean on what feels right. If it's The Universe that speaks to you and a belief that we're part of something bigger than ourselves, that's what's calling you. Regardless of beliefs, there is a force within us and around us guiding us through this life and encouraging us to follow our purpose. I will refer to God many times throughout this chapter and my story. If that's not what speaks to you, replace "God" with your beliefs. I encourage you to not get caught up in specific language because that will only prevent you from grasping the power. We were given one life and it will take this life to live out our purpose.

Making Your Inner Voice your BFF

Maybe you've felt a divine nudge before, or maybe you haven't. Regardless, these nudges are inside all of us; we just need to get quiet enough to hear them. Listening to your soul or receiving a divine nudge won't happen when you're talking or busy with life. The key to receiving these messages is to create space for them through silence, which is easier said than done these days. Most people are busy and only getting busier. We're a society that values productivity over silence and contemplation and doing over being. There's a time and place for everything, but you can't hear your inner voice without stillness and silence. We're human beings but we live like we're human doings. When we balance stillness and quiet with activity, we're more likely to be in tune with these nudges and pay closer attention to them.

I was not a quiet child growing up and I certainly wasn't

a quiet, contemplative teen or young adult. I'd always been the girl who brought the group together for shenanigans or came up with the ideas that later you look back on and say, "We really should have known better." For most of my life I considered myself an extrovert. I never liked being alone and was often the center of attention. For this reason, it's actually quite surprising I even heard these nudges at all. The concept of valuing stillness was an idea that came to me only within the last five years. Even though my parents have always said that I have a strong intuition, I never made time to tap into this power, not until I was older.

The calling to follow your heart or pursue your passion will come from within and no one will hear it but you. Most of the time it will be a tiny stirring, deep from within, encouraging the idea that you were made for something great. This voice doesn't make a sound and it doesn't have words. It will feel like this tiny piece of you that's been with you for as long as you can remember; it's fully you. It's the you that existed before other people's expectations of you. It's the you that didn't think about the "smart" career path or the one that would make the most sense. It doesn't come from a place of logic and reason. It comes from a place of authentic truth and intuition.

For some, this stirring will bring peace because it's familiar—you've felt it before. For others, it will feel uncomfortable because it's stretching you.

Think of this stirring, this inner voice, as your best friend. Except this best friend will always be there for you, never leave you for someone else, knows you completely, and always has your best interest in mind. There's never any judgment, comparison, or competition. This best friend is your best self. It's your past self, your present self, and your future self. It wants what's best for you and will nudge you to do things that are scary and uncomfortable but purposeful.

We were all born with unique and wonderful gifts. And we were placed here, in this time, and in this place, for an intended purpose. Your inner self, that little voice, is YOU. It knows why you're here and what you're called to do. It knows the life you were designed to live and what gifts you were placed on this planet with to make this a better place. There's a whole plan we're all a part of and you have a very specific, special role that no one can fill but you. This tiny voice is pushing you to uncover who that beautiful, magical person is inside.

But what you're called to do is not small. None of us was put on this planet to play small, not a single one of us. To partner with that little voice and step out into the great unknown to follow the stirring in your heart, you will need to get uncomfortable and forget about other people's opinions of you and what they think you should be doing with your life.

Most of us live every day like we have many left. We assume we'll grow old and that we have a lifetime on this planet. We put off today what can be done tomorrow and too many of us won't even try to pursue our purpose or passion because there's always another day. We spend our days getting by instead of getting ahead and we stop dreaming that we were made for more. You and I might not know one another personally, but I can tell you with one hundred percent certainty that you were made to be great. No one has your story, your background, or your unique gifts. You're the only you and the world needs you now.

Creating and Balancing Stillness

Understanding your true purpose or calling comes from within and around you. The first step in hearing your inner voice or receiving a driving nudge is slowing down and listening. This doesn't necessarily happen the instant you decide to get quiet. It happens over time as you create a space for stillness.

If you're already well-acquainted with your inner voice but haven't been listening, that's where we need to start. If, on the other hand, you have no idea what I'm talking about, we need to start there. The first step looks the same for either starting place: create stillness. Stillness is a designated time during your day that you intentionally stop doing and focus on being. This was a very foreign concept to me when I first started. I have always liked being around people and up until a few years ago, I surrounded myself with people all day, every day. I did not like being alone, but as I started reading books about successful entrepreneurs, I began picking up on reoccurring themes. One of these was creating stillness through reflection and meditation.

This idea that busy entrepreneurs prioritize meditation and stillness surprised me. Again, my internal depiction of an entrepreneur was more of the busy, important type and less of the silent, contemplative type. However, when I hear an idea multiple times, I pay attention. And eventually, as in the case of meditation, I give it a whirl myself. The results I've experienced have been nothing short of life changing.

Meditation and tapping into my inner voice have made all the difference in achieving balance as well. What I've found is that often we have the answers right inside of us, but we need to get quiet in order to hear that inner voice. When we listen to this inner voice and we find the answers living inside ourselves, it's much easier to balance the demands of everyday life. We know what's important to us and who we are which creates ease and greater peace in making difficult decisions. It also helps keep us from being pulled in too many directions, leading to greater balance in all areas of our lives.

Through these practices, I know that what I'm doing is

purposeful and in alignment with who I am at my very core. The other reason it's been powerful is because sometimes it's the only voice encouraging me through the tough stuff. Look, I have a great support network of friends and family, but sometimes well-intentioned people can give really bad advice. Knowing who you are and being able to draw upon your own voice is sometimes the only voice directing you down the right path.

Step 1 – Make Time

Plan for time in your day or throughout your day for stillness. This can be a meditation practice, devotion, prayer, or simply sitting outdoors or somewhere peaceful and just being, not doing. The biggest thing that stopped me from doing this early on was that my mind would wander and my thoughts would be all over the place. I'd be thinking about what I was going to make for dinner and what I said to someone a few days ago. It bothered me when this would happen because I thought I needed to stop the thoughts, that my stillness practice was only successful if my mind was blank. That is absolutely not the case! I've since learned that for most of us, we will experience "racing thoughts" or a busy mind and that is A-OK! The trick is that you don't need to listen to these thoughts; you can let them come in and simply let them back out, paying very little attention to them at all.

One of the first questions many people have is "How much time should I plan for?" The answer is different for everyone, but my minimum recommendation is ten minutes. Ten minutes is a pretty long time for most of us to sit without a planned agenda, but it's just enough time to reap the benefits of stillness. One day, ten minutes might fly by in the blink of an eye and on another day, it might feel substantially longer. But discipline yourself to sit for ten minutes regardless of how it feels. Set a timer on your phone or other device and wait until it goes off.

The time of day you choose is up to you and your schedule, but most people find that mornings are the easiest place to find extra time. Our minds tend to be quieter in the morning as well, which helps because we aren't fighting racing thoughts. I've found that when I incorporate this practice first thing, right before I grab a cup of coffee, it helps me focus and find peace in whatever I am doing next and throughout my day.

The key for realizing the benefits of stillness is to incorporate these moments every single day. The first time you sit down to meditate, it might feel good or you might find it frustrating. Either way, the power in the practice will come after incorporating it daily. When I first started meditation, I used an app on my phone to help guide me through a daily ten-minute practice. It took a full month before I started noticing the value of the practice and the application throughout my day. This is not a quick fix, but it can make a profound difference over time. It's very important not to judge yourself or the practice as you're getting started.

We tend to evaluate ourselves whenever we're trying something new and we're quick to judge whether we're performing well or performing poorly. Meditation is a practice and not something to be measured as good or bad. Everything you experience throughout your practice is a learning opportunity. If you find that your thoughts are racing, and you'd like to quiet your mind, that's something you can focus on in your practice—noticing your thoughts and letting them go without giving much consideration to them. You can develop this over time and it will help you throughout your day; as random thoughts try to steal your attention, simply let them go.

Meditation pulls us out of our minds and into our bodies.

We're accustomed to making decisions from a place of logic and reason, from a rational standpoint. We tend to overthink things and pride ourselves on making thoughtful decisions. Meditation helps get you out of your head and into your heart, which is where key decisions should be made. This is where your inner guide lives. You have many of the answers right within you and getting out of your head will help you get in touch with yourself again.

Your inner voice will come from this place within yourself because it is simply who you are at your very core. It won't shout at you. It will feel more like a stillness in your core, a peace that comes from deep within. When you're connected to your most authentic self, your true power radiates and you catch a glimpse of what you're truly capable of. You are powerful beyond measure. Your life is incredibly meaningful and you matter tremendously. This is the place where decisions should be made. Connecting with your inner self feels familiar because you knew this person inside and out when you were younger. You might have lost touch with her as you grew up, but she's still there and she's just as familiar as when you were younger. You can connect with your inner voice anytime throughout your day by simply breathing deeply and finding that inner peace.

One critical aspect of meditation or stillness is breath. When you find a place of peace to sit in stillness, consciously breathe from your diaphragm. Take long, slow breaths in and exhale just as slowly. This is not only therapeutic, but it will also help drown out any noises around you and within you. It will give you something to focus on instead of listening to your thoughts. Any time you find yourself distracted by thoughts, come back to the breath. If you've never focused on your breath in this way, you will be surprised by how much this will refresh your entire body. In our busy world, we've lost the very nature of proper breath. We tend to breathe shallow breaths instead of deep, cleansing breaths that fill the lungs and empty out stale air.

I heard a metaphor once that I like to think of when it comes to breathing. Think of your lungs like a glass of water that sat out on your nightstand overnight. When you pick up that glass in the morning, the water is stale from sitting out all night, so you'll likely want to dump it out and get a fresh glass of water. This is similar to the air in our lungs when we're taking shallow breaths—the air becomes stale. By taking those deep, cleansing breaths, we're able to clear out the stale air and nourish the body with fresh oxygen.

Once you've felt the power of your inner self, you'll likely want to come back to it again and might even feel frustrated on a day that you're unable to connect with this place of power. Have patience; connecting with your deepest self can be like finding a new destination on a map. At first, the route is unknown and bumpy, but the more frequently the trip is made, the easier it is to find. Taking deep breaths is the fastest way to get back on track.

Step 2 - Look for Coincidences and Things that Make You Jealous

Something odd happens when you've tapped into and you're listening to your inner voice. You'll start to pick up on messages you would have otherwise missed. These messages will come in two different forms: coincidences and jealousy.

Have you ever had a conversation with someone and then later found that same conversation popping up elsewhere with someone else? When you begin uncovering the things that light you up and get your wheels spinning, don't be surprised when they start showing up all over the place! Coincidences help us notice the small ideas taking up space within us that might not be registering on a conscious level. This is why coincidences are important to pay attention to—they help to identify our true desires.

Jealousy is another effective tool to help us discover our desires. Jealousy is not a dirty word in my dictionary. In fact, I think jealousy can be very purposeful if you use it correctly. Jealousy is simply our internal compass pointing us in the direction of our desires. The key is not letting these feelings get out of control, but to be aware of them and where they're showing up.

When it became clear to me that I needed to write this book, I started noticing people all over the place who were writing books! It seemed like everyone in my network was either writing a book or had just published a book. I recall multiple book launches that occurred while this dream sat untouched in my heart, and every single launch made me want to kick, scream, and cry like a little kid. Why? Because that's what I wanted to do, but I wasn't actually doing it.

One day, I caught myself acting like this cranky, irrational child when I was making up some story in my head about another one of the books that had launched. I was telling myself this other person's book probably wasn't good anyway and that I could write a better one. I was comparing my unwritten book to this person's published book and getting all upset about it when I realized what a jerk I was being. I was incredibly jealous of other people's accomplishments when it came to writing and publishing books because that's exactly what I wanted to be doing but wasn't actually doing.

After this realization, I course corrected. I forced myself to buy their books and celebrate their successes. I had been making the whole situation about me when it had nothing to do with me! They had accomplished something great, something

I wanted to do myself, and something that was worthy of celebration.

This is how you can turn jealousy into a force for good instead of a dirty word we try to avoid. Get curious about what's making you jealous; instead of judging it and thinking, "I shouldn't feel that way," ask yourself, "Why am I feeling jealous? What is this revealing to me about my dreams and desires?" The key is to not let these feelings take over. By getting curious and asking these questions, you'll discover what's actually going on and we can work with that.

You will likely find feelings of jealousy around other people's possessions, accomplishments, career advancement, marital status, spouses, vacations, their children, their friends, what they're eating for lunch, and their adorable Goldendoodle posted all over Instagram. Take heart; this is normal. It's also normal to try to shut these negative thoughts down because we think jealousy is dirty, when in fact, we need to be digging up the roots of their existence. Figuring out I was jealous of people who were writing books seems innocent compared to coveting someone's spouse or a purse they bought, doesn't it? But it's all important because these seeds of jealousy are planted somewhere within our deepest desires and those matter for our happiness and fulfillment.

If it's happy couples that make you cringe, that's likely coming from a deep desire for love that you're not currently receiving. If it's a purse, that's probably stemming from a lack of resources. What would need to change in order for you to find love or have the resources to treat yourself? We have the ability to shift our current situation and start making decisions and taking risks to pursue what really matters to us and our happiness. Sitting at home scrolling through social media and building up anger towards everyone and their wonderful lives isn't working, so it might be time to make a shift.

What does this have to do with meditation and belief? Meditation is tapping into our most authentic, truest selves. It's getting super clear on what you desire and why you're here. Your desires, your purpose, and your gifts are all tangled up into the same messy, colorful ball of yarn. It's not always clear where one begins and the other ends, but they're all smooshed in there together and connected. Sometimes figuring out what we desire and getting upset about why we don't have it is exactly what it takes to figure out how our lives need to shift in order to pursue a career path that opens richer possibilities.

Step 3 – Speak Life Into Your Purpose

When you get clear on what it is you want to do, be, or have, it's time to start sharing it with others. If our dreams and desires remain a secret trapped within our hearts, it's a whole lot easier for us to cover them up and pretend we never discovered them in the first place. Sharing with others is the first step in being accountable to ourselves. I know that pursuing your purpose is scary. I know it brings up a whole host of emotions and fear. That's why no one should have to walk through this alone; let people support you in this journey.

Start by creating a list of a few people who love you and want to see you live your best life. This list doesn't have to be long. It can be your mom and your best friend, but write down their names. These are your dream supporters, the people who will encourage you to pursue your calling, chase after what sets your heart on fire, and not allow you to play small.

It's important to share our dreams and desires with others even if it feels crazy and outlandish. Sharing with others does a few things. First, it opens the dream up to others and uncovers the secrecy, which allows people to support and encourage you. Second, it speaks life into your purpose. Simply verbalizing what you really want will transform you. The minute the words are on your lips, you can't take them back. For this reason alone it's a blessing that I sometimes speak before I think. When it comes to my dreams, I've found myself surprised by what I have to say, but it's also been key to pursuing my purpose. Once the words are out, you can't take them back.

Sharing with others also creates an accountability group. We often don't want to share our dreams with other humans for fear of looking stupid and the simple fact that they'll probably ask us about it, which means we'll have to make progress towards it! Pursuing your dreams does not have to be a long, painful, fear-filled slog. In fact, that's the opposite of how it should feel. Pursuing your big, hairy, audacious goals and dreams can actually be a ton of freakin' fun, if you let others in. Doing anything scary is better when you're surrounded by loving supporters. The final thing that speaking your dreams does is open the door for possibilities. If you want to start an elephant rescue in Tanzania, your friend Sam might know just the person you need to talk to. These things rarely happen in a vacuum; people will help you along your path.

Everything starts with belief. Believing that the answers can be found within us, that we're capable of pursuing our dreams and that external forces will support us on our journeys. Building your belief, tapping into your inner self and getting into action require a delicate balance that can only be learned through application. This balance is like a dance, getting still one moment to hear what's in your heart, while taking purposeful steps the next.

Journaling Prompts: Putting Pen to Paper and Getting Real

1. The idea of being a "fraud" or an "impostor" has come up twice in my story in the last two chapters. These feelings come from a place of not being prepared for the roles I was filling. As women, we tend to feel like a fraud when we don't think we're ready for the task at hand. This feeling can hold us back from pursuing roles outside of our comfort zones. Have you ever felt like a fraud? What opportunities have you resisted or are you holding yourself back from because you don't feel fully prepared?

2. Out of all four key elements of belief: gut instinct, confidence, inner voice and external forces or higher power, which one(s) do you struggle with the most? Which are strongest in your life today?

3. Show me what you're jealous of and I'll show you your true desires. We don't like admitting we feel jealous of something, someone or in certain situations but that feeling can be the key to bringing awareness to our internal desires. Take some time to journal about what makes you jealous. Don't judge the feelings; instead get super curious and ask, "what about that thing causes me discomfort?"

Taking the Lesson One Step Further with Recommended Reading

You are a Badass – How to Stop Doubting Your Greatness and Start Living an Awesome Life, by Jen Sincero

The Universe Has Your Back – Transform Fear to Faith, Gabrielle Bernstein

One Action Step to Build Momentum

Begin the process of developing a meditation practice.

- 10 minutes every day
- Mornings work best
- Schedule it on your calendar
- Commit to showing up
- Use apps or resources to support you
- Don't judge, just commit to showing up daily

CHAPTER 3

The Life Plan Comes Before the Business Plan

"When I was five years old, my mother always told me that happiness was the key to life. When I went to school, they asked me what I wanted to be when I grew up. I wrote down 'happy.' They told me I didn't understand the assignment, and I told them they didn't understand life."

—John Lennon

Sometimes Things Need to Break in Order to Be Fixed

THE BUSINESS WAS only three years old and considering that it had grown out of the recession, with little hope of quick success, we were doing quite well. Revenue was growing every month; we were making waves in local and national media, and our team was consistently expanding. But I was miserable. I had every reason to pop out of bed in the morning—to further grow the business I owned or simply collect the largest paycheck I had made up to that point, but every morning I woke up with dread.

Have you ever found yourself in a job you hated? That was my life and I owned the job; I was the owner of the business! My stomach was constantly in knots, my mind distracted with thoughts of work, and my heart felt heavy. My husband John would try to talk to me about how our daughter Wren was doing or what plans we had for the weekend, but it felt like I was a million miles away. There was this constant sinking feeling in my stomach and I was unable to make decisions. This was not the way I had imagined entrepreneurship, but then again, everyone had told me it would be difficult. I just assumed this, too, was part of the role.

We'd assembled the business quickly due to the timing in the economy. We worked off our business plan that'd we'd made in a week, making edits over the years. The business had exceeded our expectations and was growing consistently. Three years in, we had more than doubled the size of our office space by opening up a wall and were looking for new space because our current digs couldn't accommodate our growing team. On the outside, things looked great, which made my feelings of discontent feel that much more confusing. The problem came down to one simple idea I did not understand at the time: To achieve balance, your life plan must come before your business plan.

The business no longer fit the life I desired to create for myself and my family. At twenty-five years old, newly married, and without children, it had all worked perfectly. I was able to work late nights, early mornings, and every weekend, but after starting a family I knew those weren't sacrifices I wanted to make. It was during this time in my life that the importance of balance began to take root. The value of my time had changed. In my PR business I could tell you my billable hourly rate, but I could not tell you my rate for raising a family because it couldn't be quantified. I was irreplaceable in the life of my daughter.

What is a mother's time worth? In the world of business, there are financial statements that communicate the financial health of the business. Even if I felt great about the business, I could not hide from the way I was feeling at home. My thoughts were distracted; my heart was heavy; I was never truly present, and I was short-tempered. My balance sheet between work and home was out of balance, and everything I was feeling were symptoms of this problem.

Closing One Chapter to Start Another

When I realized how unhappy I was with the business, my partner was on maternity leave and we hadn't spoken in weeks. I justified our lack of communication by telling myself she needed time with her baby and that she didn't need to be bothered with work. But I could feel it and even if I wasn't admitting it to others, I couldn't ignore the feelings myself—I was disconnected from her and the business. This business wasn't lighting me up anymore. The business and the role I played as the founder and owner felt heavy. There were days at the office I would try to be productive and do the work that needed to be done, but instead I would just stare out the window at my daughter's daycare down the road. It just wasn't working and I felt trapped. I didn't know what to do.

Around this time, we were working with a business coach who helped us with employee communications and business strategy. One of the assignments she had us work on was to write a letter to ourselves five years in the future. She wanted us to think of our future selves and write a letter detailing what life was like five years down the road. It was a powerful exercise and incredibly eye-opening because as much as I tried to force myself to, I could not bring myself to write about this business. I didn't see the business in my future five years from that day.

I wrote about my family and the life we were living. We were traveling and I was spending time with my children, days that didn't feel burdened with thoughts about the business. The odd thing was that I did write about a different business I owned, not the one I was currently running. The business I owned five years into the future was something that fit within my gifts and talents. It was a creative business, one that lit me up and gave me energy instead of draining it. It was during this exercise that I realized I needed to make some difficult decisions. The business I had started was successful, but it wasn't the right business for me anymore and couldn't provide the lifestyle I desired.

One day, after a long day at work, I finally made the decision. I had picked up Wren from daycare and brought her home. Just the sight of her and her scent as I wrapped her in my arms brought on a flood of emotions like it did every time I picked her up. I teared up as I did almost every day when I was finally able see her. She was my constant reminder to never give up, to search for a balanced solution that would fit our family. Life was precious and I knew these moments wouldn't last forever. She was growing quickly; her milestones came one after another and time was slipping away like sand between my fingers.

That night, I continued to feel emotional as I made her dinner and watched as her tiny hands moved her food around her plate, getting some into her mouth but most onto the floor. I was observing her, trying to lock this moment into my memory so I would never forget it. She had already grown so much. We had celebrated her first birthday and her second was right around the corner. I found myself thinking about time. Did it always pass this quickly? Why hadn't I noticed until she came into our lives? After giving her a bath, I got her ready for bed. I loved the way her little toes pushed at the end of her footie pajamas and how her clean skin smelled almost sweetly fresh out of the tub. As we rocked in the glider and read books,

I held onto her tightly, never wanting to let her go. When I finally laid her down and made it back downstairs, I went into the living room and laid on the floor. In that moment, I was finally able to let the tears I had been holding back all night stream from my eyes.

John came over and sat down to talk to me. He wasn't a stranger to my emotions or the tension I was feeling. With tenderness and support he asked, "What do you want to do?" I hesitated. I knew the answer deep down, but it was the new house, the bills, my reputation, and simply the "how" that prevented the words from coming out. "I don't know" was all I could say. So, John said it for me: "You need to get out; I'm worried about you." And in that one statement a flood of new tears came rushing out as I leaned into him and nodded my head.

It was the "I'm worried about you" that finally tripped something in my brain. He was right; I was worried about me, too. I was on anti-anxiety and depression medications after having Wren and struggling with postpartum depression. I wasn't doing well. My time in the office moved painfully slow; the minutes crept by, and I waited to leave. Each day was getting harder to endure. When I looked at myself in the mirror, I couldn't see any life left in my eyes. I was trying to fake it, but it was obvious to everyone. My creativity, a gift I'd embraced my whole life, was gone. I had nothing to give and I was terrified of losing it all. I could see Wren getting older by the day and I was missing it. I was missing the joy and the celebration because I wasn't there. I had lost myself and was losing everything as a result.

That night something changed inside of me, and I started taking steps to make a change on the outside. The next day I emailed my business partner and asked to meet for coffee so we could talk. She responded quickly and without the typical niceties like, "I'm doing great on maternity leave. How are you?" She simply said, "That would be a good idea." We scheduled the coffee meeting for later that week, not wasting any time.

The day I walked into the coffee shop, my heart was racing and I felt sick to my stomach knowing the conversation we needed to have. We sat down and briefly chatted about the business and family, all of it feeling forced and insincere. We both knew why we were there. Sarah was the one brave enough to make the move.

"This isn't working. I don't want to be business partners with you anymore."

I drew in a sharp breath as I tried to soften the blow. I didn't want her to know how much her words stung. The truth was, I didn't want to be a part of the business anymore, but I wasn't prepared for her to tell me she didn't *want* me in the business. It felt like a childhood friend telling you they didn't want to be your friend anymore. It hurt in every part of my body. I wanted to cry. It felt unnecessarily harsh. As the words sank in, they broke my heart. Then the sadness turned to anger, and I simply said, "OK, then we need to figure this out."

We separated one month later. Ending a business partnership was the closest I've come to experiencing the trauma of divorce. We decided the price of the buyout in an accountant's office by each of us writing a price on a piece of paper. We each wrote a price that we could accept to either buy out the other or walk away from the business. We did it this way because we wanted it to feel fair, that what we would sell for we would also buy the other person's shares. When we flipped over our pieces of paper, we took the two numbers and met in the middle. That's the price I accepted to sell my shares of the business. My shares were paid out over the next three years as I started taking steps forward. I didn't know what I was going to do, but I had one example of how I didn't want work and family to mix and that was the foundation for my pursuit of balance.

Sometimes the only compass we have pointing us towards where we need to go is one that's pointing us away from where we are. I learned a lot from my first business and while it hurt to walk away, I knew it wouldn't fit in the future life I imagined. I didn't know at the time what would fit, but knowing what didn't helped me take steps.

Seasons of Life Will Change – Business Can Change and That's OK

One of the areas I've found myself stuck in, and one I see others get stuck in, is thinking things should stay exactly how they've always been. That the career we imagined growing up or in college—before starting a family, purchasing a home, and figuring out what we really want in life—will fit the lifestyle we desire. Life is a series of seasons and constant change. For many, our twenties are when we start first jobs, maybe look for or date a potential life partner, and start to figure out who we really are. We're excited about all that life has to offer and are not weighed down by doubts and fears. We're ready to take life by the horns and own it! But then, somewhere after the first or second job, we get knocked down. We start to understand all that we don't yet know. We learn that what it took to get us where we are is not what it's going to take to get us where we want to be. Reality starts to set in and it can be a harsh contrast to what we had imagined.

Our twenties are often a decade when we start to put down roots somewhere and with someone. There's a lot of personal and professional change and growth during this time. Depending on one's situation, during this period we're able to pour into our careers, work late nights, early mornings, and weekends. Even if we've identified who we want to be with and are taking steps towards that future, there's typically an ability to be selfish and focus on our careers. The primary focus during this time is oneself and what's best for us moving forward. What works in this decade and in those seasons is likely to completely change in the next decade.

It goes without saying that everyone is different. Life circumstances and situations vary drastically, so if you don't fit within the above description of someone in their twenties, that's OK. The point is that life is never stagnant. Life is in constant motion and change. You can see the best example of this by simply looking out the window or getting outdoors. When I'm feeling overwhelmed or fearful, I take a walk among the trees. Observing nature and seeing life's constant changes taking place is comforting and shows us how this all works. Accepting the continual change and making adjustments to accommodate those changes is normal.

Growing up in Wisconsin, I am no stranger to change. Seasons are a part of life in the Midwest and often help set the pace of life. Spring is a time for excitement and renewal; summer is typically busy as the sun rises earlier and sets later; fall is a season of centering and preparing, while winter is comforting and reflective. The seasons change everything in nature and the only thing that's constant is the change itself. Our lives are no different.

When I started my first company, I assumed I'd be there for many, many years. Three short years later, when the decision to sell took shape, I was mostly concerned about what other people would think. Did this mean I couldn't stick it out, that I was flaky, unreliable, and wishy-washy? I worried endlessly about what others thought and how this decision would impact the rest of my career. I worried that I wasn't a true entrepreneur and that I'd surely have to start another company in order to prove myself. But after I sold my company, I made one of the most freeing decisions of my life. It took time and working through a lot of pain and tears, but I decided to let go of other people's expectations for my life and instead follow the path my inner voice was telling me to pursue.

So many of the lies we tell ourselves or thoughts that take up valuable space in our brains are wasted on what other people think of us. We'll get into this in a later chapter, but for now the important thing to know is that the decisions we make and the changes that take place are normal, despite what other people may think. Instead of worrying about what other people think or how this will impact the rest of our lives, we need to accept that changes are a part of life. What works in one stage of life will likely not work in another and that is OK. We spend a great deal of our lives preparing for careers that should fit within our natural born gifts and talents, so when things change, it can be incredibly unsettling. But the reality is that most people will not pick a vocation in one season of life and work for forty years in that same career for the rest of their lives. Their seasons will change, life will change, and opportunities will change.

Set a Goal For the Best Life, Not the Best Career.

The current system is broken: Go to college, pick a career path, work hard for 40 years, and cross your fingers that you make it to retirement, when you can finally start enjoying your life. That concept is called the deferred life plan and people no longer want to follow it. We want to enjoy life now, while we're living it. Lifestyle design is the idea that you can create the life you want to live now instead of deferring that ideal life for your later years.

We can attribute the spread of lifestyle design to social media. We're able to get a snapshot into other people's lives in a way that wasn't possible prior to the internet. You would have had to have a conversation with someone to find out how they spent their time on a daily basis to understand how they lived. Now, we can open Instagram, Facebook, and YouTube to see that people aren't following the deferred life plan anymore. They're traveling all over the world now with kids in tow, working from wherever they want, when they want. How and when did this happen?

People are deciding how they want to live before choosing what they want to do or be, which is a fundamental shift. In the deferred life plan, college is the starting point to determine the career path one will take and pursue. People choose careers based on income potential, family backgrounds, personal interests, natural born gifts and talents, and a host of other factors, but rarely do people choose careers based on life goals and how they want to live.

When I was graduating from college with a degree in advertising, I was excited about working in a swanky downtown advertising agency. The thrill of agency life seemed sexy, important, and thrilling. I wasn't thinking about how that career would fit once I had a family or whether or not it would give me the flexibility and balance that I desired later in life.

In the marketing industry, the common structure is a fee-for-service model. This means that marketing professionals have a value assigned to their time and the amount of time required to carry out their services is what they can charge for their time. You're trading time for money. I learned very quickly that unless I figured out a way to sell something besides my time and talent or own a business that sold other people's time, the model would never be a fit for me. I figured out early that trading time for money wasn't going to produce the type of income I desired or the flexible lifestyle I craved.

The same can be true for those in other professions, like

teaching or nursing, for example. At first the idea of having summers off and working with youth as a teacher seems like a great gig! Or, for the nurse, working with people and taking care of those who need support sounds rewarding and fulfilling. But being on your feet all day or dealing with constantly changing hours, or politicians that change the pay structure for an entire industry, people get to decide if the career fits their lifestyle. In both cases, there are reasons people choose these career paths, but there are also reasons people change their minds once they start in their fields. Look, I'm not advocating for people to leave these fields. We absolutely need nurses and teachers but for some people, they decide it's no longer the right fit when they start in these careers, and that's OK. There are also highly specialized fields for which a lot of education is required and a long career path is assumed. Some of those folks also might find themselves in a position where their chosen career path no longer fits their ideal lifestyle and that's OK, too!

I am personally grateful for my years in college and the degrees I now carry, but I wouldn't give them credit for the life I've created since. For many like me, college is a great next step after high school. College helped me dream bigger and truly think about my life and what I wanted to do. I started out as a Spanish major, transitioned to pre-med, and eventually ended up in communications because I liked public speaking. There are many students who take a similar route through school, bouncing around from one major to another until they land in a series of classes that align with their gifts and talents and that's where they stick. I am not advocating against going to college, though many will argue for that. I am simply saying that the career path that you choose in your late teens or early twenties may not fit the life you live in your thirties or forties.

Current student loan debt is at an all-time high, estimated at over $1.48 trillion, more than $620 billion more than U.S.

credit card debt. Couple this with the fact that, as it stands, our national social security system is in trouble and is not set up to handle the amount of people who will eventually draw on the social security system for retirement. Again, I am not making that argument that people should not go to college; I don't want to cause a fight around the dinner table about the importance of continuing education for our youth. For many, college is a dream and that's wonderful. What I am arguing and what the numbers are telling us is that it's not the "end-all be-all." Earning a degree is not the only path to a successful, balanced life and it also isn't a guarantee. The world is changing quickly, and the way people are making money around what they enjoy doing is changing just as quickly.

I remember when it was earth-shattering news to learn that Perez Hilton was making more money than most surgeons by poking fun at celebrities online. Today we have people creating careers on Twitch playing video games while others watch them! Did you catch that? There are people making careers out of playing video games all day while others watch them; I'm not joking. All over the internet, you can find examples of people taking their passions and influence online and turning them into careers. Ain't nobody going to college to learn how to play video games better, just sayin'.

Creating the Lifestyle

Determining how you want to live takes time, and today, many people will transition through multiple careers instead of staying with one career the rest of their lives. College and additional schooling are not the only means of learning and making transitions. Google, YouTube, and countless online resources provide information to help those making a shift. Gone are the days when one would need to go back to school to learn a new craft. Now you can simply watch some YouTube videos to learn what's necessary to start you off in a whole new direction.

If things are changing at an ever-increasing rate and what we used to rely on for a safe, comfortable future is shifting and people are making money in radical ways, how are we to keep up? The simple answer is that you don't need to keep up, but you do need to expand your perception of what's possible and know that whatever you desire is out there waiting for you.

But first it starts with you and your life. How do you want to live? What does a balanced, fulfilled, purpose-driven life look like for you? Will you have a family? If so, how large will that family be and where will you raise your family? Do you want to live in one house or travel around the world, living in many locations? It's not only possible, but it's being proven all over the world that you can live how you want to live and make a living doing something you enjoy. But it starts with clarifying your desires for your life.

Imagine if the purpose of college was to determine how to live your best life instead of picking a career path. What if the college years were filled with getting clear on what lights you up, what your unique gifts and talents are, and then visualizing how you're going to pursue your passions using your gifts to live your greatest life? For some, this may have been their college experience, but for many of us it was an extension of school where you had to pick what career you were going to pursue for the rest of your life. That's a big decision to make if it's your first time living on your own and away from your family.

It's tough to figure out in college or early in our lives how we desire to live. Sometimes we don't know how we want to live until we're getting it wrong. Until we're in a situation where we think, "I thought there was more to life than this." That's when we have the option to change and make decisions based on how we want to live and what we want to do. I'm a big believer in the "and" not the "or." We hear throughout our lives that you can have this or that. You can have a high-paying job or you can have flexibility. You can stay at home with your kids and raise them or you can have a fulfilling career. I don't buy this school of thought; I believe in the "and." You can have a fulfilling, high income career AND raise your children how you choose with the flexibility to live how you want to live. The key is deciding how you want to live and what lights you up, and pursuing balance in the midst of that.

The Thing that Lights You Up is the Thing You Were Meant to Follow

We're taught to be reasonable, to pick a respectable path that will provide enough income to live a comfortable life. Most career counselors are doing the best job they can in guiding students to make smart decisions and keep parents happy. They aren't necessarily spreading the message that life is short and we've got one shot at this sucker so make it everything you can imagine. That sounds awfully risky and uncertain. As humans, we desire stability and certainty, yet somewhere, somehow, we're lit up by spontaneity and excited about ambiguity. We're walking contradictions and you can see these contradictions play out in career choices and options.

I remember being in college, wanting to pick a career path that would make my parents proud. I was always a good kid, mostly a B-average student, but I had a wild side and my parents knew it. Throughout my childhood, they reinforced that I would be successful in whatever I chose, but they weren't certain what that would be. My mom thought I would be an entertainment director on a cruise ship, if that gives you any idea as to what they thought my gifts and talents were. I've always wanted to make them proud and surprise them by being responsible and consistent, but somewhere inside I knew success was going to look different for me.

What if instead of making career decisions based on stability, logic, and reason, we made decisions based on what gets our wheels spinning, what lights us up? What is that thing that keeps you up at night or pulls you from your bed in the morning? What's the thought that comes back time and time again that causes you to wonder, "What if?" Those little nudges are our inner voice; those thoughts that flutter in the back of our minds that cause us to say, "someday maybe I can do something with that" are the very things we need to pursue now! You've heard it before and I'll say it again: there is no someday. You cannot wait for the perfect time to act. The perfect time does not exist and is not a guarantee. Life is a precious gift, one that we cannot take for granted. I learned that when we lost my brother so unexpectedly. You are here, at this moment in time, for a purpose and on purpose. No one has your story, your background, your gifts, or your talents, and the world needs you to pursue that inkling tugging on your heart.

The day I completed the exercise of writing a letter to my future self five years down the road, do you know what business I thought I'd own? I thought I would own an interior design business. Those who know me know I am incredibly passionate about environments. I have more coffee table books on design than any other subject matter. My entire core changes when I see a beautiful, well-designed space. I love it so much I light up! So, after I sold my company, I decided to intern with an interior design firm to get my feet wet before making the decision to head back to school.

What I learned might seem heartbreaking, but it really wasn't. I hated it. I hated everything about it. I hated going to wealthy people's homes and steaming their curtains or karate-chopping their pillows into just the perfect form. I learned that while I loved designing my own spaces, I did not like spending my time doing it for others. So, I never went back to school for interior design and I continued forward. There's absolutely nothing wrong with exploring one career path only to discover it's not a fit. In fact, this helps to provide further clarity and direction. Knowing what we don't want is just as important as what we do, and sometimes that's the best guide.

Have you ever started a sentence like this: "This might sound crazy, but . . ."? Or thought to yourself: "I don't know if it's possible, but I would sure love to . . ."? These thoughts come from your heart, your soul, and the deepest part of who you are. The crazier it sounds the better. It should be crazy. It should almost make you cringe and wrinkle your nose because the thought of it just seems impossible. I'm here to tell you that is good! That's the thing you need to pursue and here's the deal: you do not need to know how. You do not need to know the plan or how it will play out. It's virtually impossible to understand it all. Remember, the path is created with every step you take. If you see the whole path, it's someone else's and not yours. This is what can make following our calling and our passions so scary and uncertain; we're creating it as we live it with every step.

This stirring in your soul is also not financial. Money will come later. In the beginning, it's all about what lights you up. Don't get stuck in the financial spiral of trying to figure out how you're going to monetize these gifts. Take small steps in the direction of what gets you excited and when your brain starts thinking about money or time or how this isn't going work, shut it down. Consciously choose to stop the spin. The very fact that your brain is freaking out is actually a good thing, which we'll get into more in a later chapter. This is how we're wired.

Instead of asking why, just know that's how it is. If you're coming up with a million objections about why this will never work, you know you've found your thing. Congratulations!

Decide and Pivot!

How do you find this thing that lights you up? In my experience, it's actually the thing right in front of your face. It's so obvious, it's easy to miss. It's the thing you would do for free because you love it. It's the thing you have a strong opinion about when the conversation comes up. It's the thing that causes you envy when you see other people doing it and crushing it. Quite simply, it stirs something inside of you. It might even make you ugly when it makes you jealous. Remember, that's a clue! That's it! That's your thing.

If you're still confused or unsure, there are a couple of ways you can gain clarity around your thing. Meditation is huge. If you've never spent an extended period of time getting out of your head and into your soul, that's the first step. Take 10 minutes each day to sit with your eyes closed, breathe intentionally, and see what comes up. Don't expect an answer to jump out at you in the first session; that's not how it works. What you're practicing and learning to do is how to listen to your innermost self. You're learning how to get out of your head—the driver of being realistic, the dream killer—and learning how to get into your heart and soul, the essence of who you are, your truth. Your purpose will come from your heart, not your head.

Another great tool I've used many times throughout my life is journaling. Have you ever had the experience of journaling your thoughts and feelings and been surprised by what comes up? Journaling tends to do that. Journaling is so powerful when we're letting out our thoughts and feeling, just free flowing out of the pen onto the paper. It helps relieve stress by getting racing thoughts out of our heads and can be a powerful gateway for opening up our hearts. The cool thing is that if you practice this consistently, you will also start to see trends. Your thing will start to take shape when you read back what you've written.

The other thing to start doing is to pay attention to what others say about you. Ask your mom or your dad what you were like as a child. What things did you do for fun? What did they think you'd be when you got older? Ask your friends, colleagues, and family what they see as your gifts. As you start to gather these thoughts and ideas, it won't necessarily make your purpose crystal clear, but it will start giving you clues leading you towards that purpose.

I have always been creative. I was the kid that chose art projects over toys. Even though it wasn't always clear how this creativity would present itself in my career, it's been a necessary element for feeling fulfilled in my work. My creativity has taken the form of writing, business planning, marketing and communications plans, videos, photos, and countless other things that light me up and let my creative wheels spin!

Lastly, I will remind you to pay attention to weird, coincidental things that happen. If you ever think, "That was coincidental," just know that it wasn't and that you should pay attention to it. Also, if there are things that you think or say that seem odd at the time, those are things to pay attention to as well.

Let me give you an example. This isn't going to paint me in the best light, but I think it'll be valuable so I'm willing to divulge. A couple of years ago, one of my closest friends threw herself a themed birthday party. She rented a bus and we all dressed up in a combination of '80s, punk rock, and cowgirl attire to visit various hole-in-the-wall bars via said bus. Somewhere during the course of the night, we thought it would be a good idea to dance in the moving bus on the seats. During my window-shattering rendition of a country song about buying a boat with a yeti cooler, I fell into another friend, hitting my cheekbone on her forehead. The next morning, I woke up with a beautiful black and blue eye that spread down my cheek. When I called my friend to tell her what I was seeing in the mirror, I said with relief, "Thank goodness I'm not a public speaker!" That, folks, was a little insight I needed to pay attention to. The truth was I knew deep down I wanted to speak but I wasn't doing it. After I got the black eye, I decided to pursue public speaking and recognized some things about my current lifestyle that would need to change in order to support this dream.

This whole process of discovering what lights you up is incredibly fun! Is it scary? Yup, but excitement and fear feel exactly the same way; choose excitement and reinforce this choice with the words you speak out loud. When we trust our hearts and get out of our heads, everything feels more peaceful, lighthearted. You'll know you're making the right shift when you feel lighter, hopeful, and excited. You may even feel a little giddy or silly because you know you're on a purposeful path and you feel like you have the best-kept secret. Don't be surprised when you can't quite explain it to others or when you try to and they look at you perplexed. Remember, it's not about what other people think; everyone has their unique timing and circumstances. Your job is to keep attracting good into your life, so make sure you're having fun during this time.

Above all else, take care of yourself. That's right, I said it. This is where balance comes in. I know you have responsibilities and maybe other people who rely on you, but this is the time for the oxygen mask. We're taking care of you first, so you can be your absolute best, most fulfilled self for others. Prioritize self-care and do things you enjoy that also make life a little more fun. When you're having fun, you will attract the greatest people and new opportunities into your life. This will ensure that you're living your best, most balanced life.

Thinking Like an Entrepreneur, Not an Employee

The mindset it takes to build a thriving business is the same one you need to cultivate to take control of your life, to go after your "and" rather than your "or." This mindset is that of an entrepreneur and if you don't feel like you already have it, you can develop it. Maybe you're already an entrepreneur. You may already have a business and know what it takes to run and grow that business. That's great; you've got a head start! If you don't, that's perfectly OK, too; everyone has to start somewhere and everyone started at some point.

Most of us were employees before we became entrepreneurs. The employee mindset shows up in more places than just at work; it shows up in the rest our lives, too. I felt it when I started my company. No one was telling me when and where to show up or what to do; it was all up to me and it was an adjustment. An employee is someone who earns an income through doing work for someone else. When you're an employee, you ultimately report to someone else who employs you. You have a job to perform that entails certain responsibilities and tasks, and when you're done, an exchange of income occurs. As an employee, someone else assigns your responsibilities to you. You may have the ability to choose how you do them and make changes, but ultimately you were hired into a specific role. You report to someone else who makes sure you're performing your job adequately. This person or company has the ultimate say in when you get paid and how much. It's important to outline all of this because it has a profound impact on your mindset.

The employee mindset also impacts our sense of validation.

Everyone likes getting confirmation that they've done a job well and their work meets expectations. But this feedback loop for an entrepreneur looks very different from an employee. In the employee's world, the feedback typically comes from a manager or a company officer during a review or check in process. For the entrepreneur, that validation must come from oneself and eventually from successful revenue growth. Feedback typically happens faster for the employee versus the entrepreneur, who may not see that validation until revenue increases.

Permission-seeking is also a common practice in employment. A boss would like you to ask for permission before proceeding with a big idea because if it's utilizing resources (time and money) she will want to make sure you're making the right choices. Asking for permission starts even before employment begins. Think about the hiring process. You're basically asking for permission to do a job by submitting all the reasons you think you're qualified (résumé), sitting down with the decision-maker while they ask you questions (interview), and then they decide whether or not you may proceed with the job. Very few people look at the responsibilities of a job and start to perform them before getting the job. We seek permission to do the job and then perform the work.

In the entrepreneurial world, this is completely backwards. The entrepreneur performs the work well before others approve of what she's building. In many cases, people will actually tell the entrepreneur she's crazy and that the risk isn't worth it. People tend to shy away from the person who's bucking the whole system and going out on her own. Permission and validation in entrepreneurship come from within, from a belief in oneself that your ideas are important and that you're capable of creating the life you desire. That can be an uncomfortable shift for the person accustomed to receiving this from others.

In addition to permission and validation, an employee is

typically contained within a time and responsibility parameter. Employees are told what they need to do in order to do their job well and when they need to do it. They're expected to be at work between certain hours during the week with a predetermined amount of time off each year. Even for virtual employees, they have expectations associated with the job they were hired to do. The work needs to be performed to earn the money they desire. There is no such thing for an entrepreneur, especially for one creating a new business. The area where most entrepreneurs fall flat is in managing their own time, knowing what needs to be done in what time, and doing it consistently.

The first step is for the entrepreneur to organize her free time. Unlike the employee, the entrepreneur doesn't have the structure and the schedule in place when setting up a business, so it's on her to create this structure and stick to it! This in and of itself can be a huge challenge for someone who's not familiar with doing this. To build a business, certain tasks need to be performed on a consistent basis to build something from nothing and those tasks will likely be more challenging to perform. We all have things we don't want to do, but for the entrepreneur, these are typically the most important tasks that need to be done, the ones that move the needle. When you don't have someone breathing down your neck, it's a whole lot easier to avoid these tasks and instead turn on *The Real Housewives* of whatever county on TV.

The last big shift in entrepreneurial thinking is in income creation instead of income earning. For most people, when they think about the scariest thing about being an entrepreneur, it's the instability of income. We've been taught or conditioned to think that a salary or a paycheck is more secure, safe, reliable, and predictable than self-employment or commission. Prior to the recession, we were also taught that corporations were more secure than small businesses. Some people still believe this to be true, but many have shifted their thinking after the countless layoffs that took place then and since. The world is changing faster today than 100 years ago, thanks to the speed of technology. It will continue to change even faster from here on out. What we used to consider safe and secure has shifted and with it our thinking needs to change. No job, company, or business is 100% safe or secure. Security is an illusion. And yet as humans, we seek safety and security. We want to know that our jobs are secure, that our income will continue coming in day after day. And even though we fundamentally understand the deferred life plan model is dying, we still desire to know that we'll have the same or increasing income year after year. Entrepreneurship is scary because it appears to be the least secure, but in the end it's actually the most secure. Once you understand how to generate your own income, you'll never need to rely on someone else or a job to provide that for you. Talk about security!

Becoming the Entrepreneur

The biggest shift from employment to entrepreneurship is not what most people fixate on—the grand idea or the starting of a business. It's the mental shift; it's thinking like an entrepreneur. If you're going to create your best, most balanced life, the grandest vision you can dream for how you want to live, where and with whom, you're going to need to think like an entrepreneur. No one will give you the plan, hold you accountable, or convince you that you're capable. That all has to come from you.

In order to take control of the reins of your life, you need to be in the driver's seat. It will be uncomfortable; you will make mistakes, but you can do it. The best part about entrepreneurship is that once you make the shift and you know you can rely on yourself to create your best life, it's the most secure place to be. No one can take that away. No one can tell you you're worth a certain amount or that you're fired because you get to make that call. If you want to earn more, you serve more, and you become more.

On the surface, entrepreneurship looks unstable because you're creating your income but it's actually more stable because the person creating your income is YOU. Do you know why people who win the lottery typically lose it all within a few years and end up worse off than when they started? Because they haven't grown into the person whose worth is that of a lottery winner. When you become an entrepreneur, you start to grow. Your income increases as you grow and when you want to increase your income, you grow. It's a simple concept with profound outcomes.

"It's simple arithmetic: Your income can grow only to the extent that you do."

—T. Harv Eker

Journaling Prompts: Putting Pen to Paper and Getting Real

1. We open up the chapter talking about how sometimes things need to break in order to be fixed. Going through struggle is not easy and it's something we'd rather avoid, but it can also be the breakthrough we've been praying for. Can you think of a time in your life where something broke? Are you facing something right now that looks like a break but might actually be a blessing?

2. Finish this sentence, "This might sound crazy but . . ."

Taking the Lesson One Step Further with Recommended Reading

The 5 Second Rule, by Mel Robbins

One Action Step to Build Momentum

Write yourself a letter 5 years down the road. I've created a document to help you walk through this powerful exercise. Keep in mind this was THE exercise that gave me clarity on selling my business. If you commit yourself to being honest and allowing yourself to dream, this exercise can be just as powerful for you. Please visit my website, https://jessdennis.com/downloads to download the guide.

CHAPTER 4

Assembling Your Winning Team

"Two people are better off than one, for they can help each other succeed. If one person falls, the other can reach out and help. But someone who falls alone is in real trouble."
—Ecclesiastes 4 : 9-10

Letting the Dust Settle

AFTER WALKING AWAY from my company, I felt utterly lost. I questioned who I was, what I wanted to do next, and who my people were. Selling the business was difficult from an identity standpoint but excruciating from a social standpoint. The people I had spent the last few years of my life with, my partner and our employees, were suddenly ripped from my life and I didn't have anyone to replace them with. I had been miserable and knew I needed a change but after the sale was final, I was caught off guard by the loneliness that followed. During the three years I had spent building the business, I was all in; working nights, weekends, and every spare moment. I had neglected friendships and other meaningful relationships to put all my energy into the business. Now that the business was gone, and with it the friendships, I had no other real relationships outside of family.

Because there were no other options on the table, I tried my hand at staying home with our daughter. I thought that because I missed her so much while working, it made sense to enter the stay-at-home-mom world. I attended mom and me classes, play times at the local YMCA, story time at the library, and music classes at a local mom and pop shop. As hard as I tried, I had a sinking feeling this wasn't for me either. I missed my work. It was during this phase that I fully embraced the fact that work is meaningful for my life. I'm a better mom and wife when I also have a career that fulfills me. Once I realized this, I opened myself up to opportunities of any form: employment, volunteering, business opportunities; anything that would help me get my feet back underneath me.

Who Got You Here Won't Get You There

The people who surround you can make all the difference between success and failure in your life. If you surround yourself with people who are enthusiastic and chasing their own dreams, you'll likely follow suit. If you surround yourself with people who complain about work but don't take any action to change it, you may find yourself in their same boat. Our peer groups have the ability to stretch our vision of what's possible or allow us to remain complacent. If we see others pursuing their dreams and refusing to settle for the status quo because they know there's more out there for them, we will probably do the same and know we'll be supported.

Even though we understand how people influence our lives tremendously, we don't always consider that when choosing who we're going to allow in or who can stay. We choose people who are like us, people we have fun with, and people who make us laugh and entertain us. We typically don't seek out people who challenge or intimidate us because we don't believe we're quite at their level. But one of the greatest secrets among some of the most successful leaders is consciously choosing the right people.

Did you know that the quickest path to success is following others? It's true. You don't need to come up with a game plan yourself and try to execute it on your own. Nope, you can quite literally find someone who's doing what you want to do but is a few steps ahead and follow them. Some call this mentorship, but it's simply following the leader. It doesn't have to be a formal process; it's just figuring out a way to spend time with someone who has what you want or is on the path you desire. That's it.

Most of us have multiple peer groups. We might have people we work with, friends we hang out with on weekends, workout buddies, a church group, fellow school parents, or any number of groups. All of these groups play a role for us and shape a part of our life. When considering who is shaping your life, it's important to consider all of these groups and identify what role they are playing and whether or not you like their influence.

The Law of Attraction in Action

Have you ever had the experience of seeing someone from a distance, maybe someone you know or even a complete stranger, and you find yourself captivated by their presence? You can see from the outside that they have something you're missing or you notice a peace about them that you desire but don't currently possess? I had this experience with someone, and I believe she was placed into my life at a very critical time. I knew of her and a little bit about her, but I had never actually talked with her. Regardless, something was pulling me towards her. Her name was Anna and I was curious about her. From what I understood, she had a big heart, loved God, and did a lot to serve the community.

Anna was one of those people that everyone seemed to know except me. Multiple friends casually mentioned her name to me and quickly followed with, "You should meet her; I think you two would get along really well." After hearing this enough, I reached out to her and asked if she would be open to having coffee with me. She enthusiastically accepted my invitation and we met at a small coffee shop near her home soon after. As she walked in, the first thing I noticed about her was her smile. She had this smile that lit up her entire face and made me feel immediately at ease. We both ordered our drinks and sat down. Our conversation was effortless, easy, like talking to a friend I had known for years. I asked her all sorts of questions about her life and she surprised me by being just as curious about mine. I liked her. I wanted to have more of her in my life, but I didn't quite know what that would look like.

Towards the end of our conversation, she mentioned that she needed to get going because she was off to her Bible study group.

I wrinkled my brow and asked, "What's a Bible study group?"

She very casually replied, "Oh, it's a group of ladies I meet with every Wednesday morning for an hour and a half. We talk about all things relating to faith."

I was shocked, an hour and a half on a Wednesday morning?! Didn't she work? Who can meet for an hour and a half every Wednesday morning and what could you possibly discuss?

She continued, "We support and challenge one another in

our faith journeys. It's a great group of women; you should come."

Sometimes I do this thing where I'm thinking one thing, in this case: "Nope, never ever," but what comes out of my mouth is the complete opposite. It's like my brain and my mouth are disconnected.

I shook my head no and said, "I'd love to; that sounds interesting."

"Great!" she replied. "I'll shoot you the details for next week."

We said our goodbyes and as she walked out the door, I sat stunned, wondering what I had just agreed to but also savoring the fact that she had invited me in the first place. It felt like an honor. Prior to our meeting, I had no interest in a Bible study group, and I still didn't even fully understand what the purpose of the group was or what the commitment looked like. Would I need to attend every Wednesday? What would John say when I told him I was choosing to attend a Bible study group instead of work every Wednesday morning for an hour and a half!? I decided I would take it one step at a time and not get too far ahead of myself. I probably wouldn't like the group anyway, so I didn't need to worry about any sort of long-term commitment.

The following week, I drove twenty minutes out of town into a tiny community where I found a tall, ornate church right off the main drag. The church stood towering over the little town, clearly the tallest building in town and probably one of the first. Growing up in the Lutheran church, I have always admired the lavish architecture of Catholic churches that stand in stark contrast to the more modern, lackluster buildings of newer Lutheran churches. I had always wanted to attend a beautiful church such as this one, if only for the sole purpose of having a beautiful wedding. The church we were married at looked more like a mushroom—round with a squatty roof, quite the opposite of this cathedral standing in front of me.

I had spent the entire twenty minutes of my drive to this tiny town questioning my sanity and decision-making ability and seeing this intimidating structure wasn't helping. I sent Anna a text as soon as I pulled into the parking lot, praying she had arrived and would be waiting for me to walk in: "Are you here?"

My phone immediately buzzed with a reply: "No, I'm on my way. Just go in, I'm running 10 minutes late."

For a moment, I debated coming up with an excuse as to why this wasn't going to work out. I had a work meeting that popped up last minute or a project I had just found out about. But lying in the parking lot of the church of God felt like the wrong decision. Plus, I swear the church was staring back at me, judging me, and watching me to see what I'd do. So, I turned off my car, took a deep breath, and stepped out. I walked slowly up to the towering church, counting my steps, willing myself to keep putting one foot in front of the other until I approached the main doors and stepped inside.

It was quiet and as I scanned the entry for a sign or something indicating where I should go, I heard faint voices coming from upstairs. There was a stairwell off to the left-hand side that appeared to lead up to the second floor. As I walked up the stairs, my mind continued to race with thoughts of doubt and ways to turn around.

At last I reached the room where the voices were coming from and as I timidly peeked into the room, my feet following behind me, I was greeted by five other women about my age, some a little older, all gathered around a conference table. They acknowledged me with smiles on their faces.

"Anna told us you would be coming. My name is Kim, welcome," said a woman who appeared to be the ringleader.

"Hi, I'm Jess," I said as I shook her hand.

Everyone else followed in introducing themselves and Kim said, "Don't mind Anna, she's always late. We'll get started without her." Luckily, Anna had shared with me the book they were working from so I had purchased it ahead of time and had done my best to catch up before the meeting.

We spent the hour and a half taking turns reading aloud from a book and engrossed in conversation about the topic for that week. I was fascinated by the depth and honesty of the discussion. I felt honored that these ladies allowed me to sit in on this private gathering where they shared their hearts with openness and vulnerability. Nowhere in any other part of my life was I having conversations like these. I felt at ease with them. I didn't understand everything they were discussing, but I liked how different their points of view were from mine. We were all women of roughly the same age but entirely different. All of my thoughts and conversations during that time in my life had been about work. After selling my company I was searching for that next thing, that next company. I was entirely focused on work. They were entirely focused on family, faith, God, sisterhood, and love. It felt like an alternate universe.

The hour and a half flew by and before I knew it, it was time to leave. I left that day smiling. My heart was full and my soul felt at peace. I didn't understand why but I felt as though I was supposed to be there. I called John on the way home and told him what I had experienced. He was happy for me and encouraged me to go back the following week. The thoughts started creeping in: How I was going to make this work? Wasn't I supposed to be figuring out my next career move? How was I going to balance everything? But I pushed those thoughts aside for now; I wanted to see these ladies again and to take it one step at a time.

I attended the following week and the weeks after that. I never planned on tapping into my faith during this stage in my life but that's exactly what I needed. Anna and this Bible study group were preordained into my life. There is zero doubt in my mind that this was not by accident. A few weeks after I started connecting with this group, Erik passed away. I don't know what it would have been like had I not known this group, but I shudder to imagine. Only because of this group did I know exactly what to do. I prayed and leaned into faith and the following week I went to Bible study.

When I walked into the room that Wednesday following Erik's death, they met me with more love, support, and compassion than I'd ever seen modeled from a peer group up to that point. They had prayed for me and my family and I could see by the compassion in their eyes that they were hurting for us.

Kim looked at me with tears in her eyes and to my shock, she said, "I actually knew Erik. I worked with him back in the day and I'm so sorry for your loss."

I immediately started crying. How could this woman, who I didn't know just two months ago and who had fully embraced and welcomed me into her circle, have known my brother? It felt like a gift. She became one of the people who now hold a very special place in my heart—the people who knew Erik. Their memories of him, no matter how big or small, mean so much to me because they knew him and through them, his memory lives on.

Unexpected Blessings

Have you had the experience of thinking of someone randomly and then receiving a call from them? This has happened to me more times than I can count, and I believe these connections are not by accident. This is how people come into our lives during seasons that we need them. We may not know we need them or understand why they're coming into our lives at that particular time, but usually we can reflect back afterwards and put the pieces together. Anna was one of those people for me. The events that have transpired in my life as a result of her influence are astounding. It has been over five years since that first Bible study meeting and I continue to attend to this day, every single Wednesday for an hour and half. The location has changed through the years and so have the people, but it continues to be a group of faithful women who love and support one another.

Too often we make the mistake of only strategizing about professional relationships, like I did. I was on a path to figure out my next career move after selling my company. I was looking for other like-minded entrepreneurs and movers and shakers. I was attending community events, networking on social media sites, and scheduling coffee meetings with community leaders. This is why Anna's pull was so confusing at the time. She didn't fit the mold of who I was looking for in my circle, but she ended up bringing exactly what I needed. Whether it's a time of transition or growth, we tend to be open to new relationships when we're moving. It might be moving professionally, personally, or simply feeling unsettled with where we are, but accepting new people into our lives means having both awareness and vulnerability.

Bringing in the New Means Moving on From the Old

Talking about bringing new people into our lives is exciting. We want people in our lives that light us up and encourage us to pursue that crazy idea we've talked about for years or take

the trip we've delayed! We want friends that live fulfilled lives
and inspire us to grow. But the scariest thing about evaluating
our friends and peer groups is that not everyone can stay.
At different points in my growth journey, this concept has
held me back. I love my friends, even the ones that complain
a little too much and never seem to do anything about their
frustrations. Friends are friends because they know us, we've
done life with them, there's history. Even if they're not the best
influences, they're comfortable and we like comfortable. But
we can't escape the truth that we are the sum of the people who
surround us and the ones who get more air time have a greater
influence.

We may tolerate that friend who always seems to have cynical
remarks about people pursuing their dreams or doesn't believe
that life can be lived to its fullest, on one's own terms. We may
just think it's fine because that's how she's always been and it's
not a big deal. But it will become a bigger deal the more you
grow and this can be scary. It's uncomfortable when you start
to have less and less tolerance for the negative viewpoints and
attitudes of the people closest to you. I've gone through very
lonely periods in my life because the peer group surrounding
me wasn't going to support me in reaching for that next level
and that's where I desired to grow.

When you grow, you will feel the shift. There will be people,
maybe not as close to you, who are incredibly supportive of
your vision and aspirations, while others who are very close to
you may suddenly feel cold or standoffish. We would naturally
assume that our closest friends would be thrilled for us if
we're pursuing dreams or creating new habits that support a
better future. But the problem is that many people cannot see
our change for what it is and simply be happy for us. Some
people, usually the ones closest to us, will see our changes and
immediately reflect themselves in those changes. They will see

our growth and for them, it will shine a spotlight on how they are not growing. This reflection is what inhibits people from being supportive and happy for us.

When boiled down, this reflection is nothing more than comparison and comparison is ugly! Comparison is any time that you see something that someone else has, does, achieves or experiences and you make it about you. This is different than jealousy because jealousy is usually a feeling of wanting what someone else has. Comparison is when we turn that around and make it about us. When we do this, we hurt ourselves the most. We see what they have or achieved and think, "I could never have that thing or do that thing because I'm lesser than." When comparison is around, nothing good can be felt; it is the thief of all joy.

Unfortunately, it's also a part of life and something we need to work hard on rewiring in our brains. Comparison has two ugly sides of the coin: it either makes us feel better or worse about ourselves. We might see someone killing it in something we desire to do ourselves, feel like we're not doing enough, and then feel crummy about our circumstances. Or, on the flip side, we might see someone who's doing what we're doing but not as well, and it might make us feel good. Either way, we're taking someone else's accomplishments and journey and making it about us, which, if you think about it, is a very selfish act at the core.

This exact same thought process is what our friends and network go through when we start to change. The human condition is to reflect oneself against others and when someone starts outgrowing the group, they're usually the one pushed out because their changes make the others feel inferior and no one likes to feel inferior. It's not fair, but it's life and this can be a very unexpected, disheartening realization. Some people may see our changes and be inspired themselves, and that's great, but for the others we'll need to actively seek out new players.

Your Five People

"You are the average of the five people you spend the most time with."

—Jim Rohn

This Jim Rohn quote is one that many professionals talk about and one that caused me to think a lot about the people in my life. There are a couple of ways this quote can be interpreted: literally and categorically. Let me explain. For a long time, I've accepted the five-person rule in a literal sense, looking at the five people I spend the most time with. In some stages of life, this is possible. When I started my first company, I spent the most time with my business partner, my husband, and our employees. They all helped shape and form my experiences at that time in my life. As life went on and John and I started a family, the quote was harder for me to understand in a literal sense because three of my people were John and the girls. I used to joke that if I started acting like an irrational toddler it was simply the influence of my peer group.

Through the years I've created a different interpretation of the rule, one that fits the various stages of life. I decided to look at the five people categorically and make sure that my categories were in alignment with my values. John and the girls are still the people who most closely surround my life. It is a blessing that I am able to spend as much time with them as I do, and they are the key players in my family category. I make sure that every week I have the appropriate amount of time allotted to spend meaningful time with them.

Another critical category for me is the faith category. My

Bible study is the group that fills this category and the group I intentionally spend time with every single week. There's a health category, which encompasses all things relating to health. I work out daily so it's important to me that the people I spend time with during those workouts are people that contribute to my life in a positive way. When looking for a facility and trainer, I consider their personalities because I will be spending a lot of time with these people and want to make sure their influence is positive. I have left more than one gym because the owner or trainer wasn't in alignment with my values and priorities inside and outside the gym.

The last two categories at this stage in my life are professional and personal development/growth. Professional relationships are those I have with other entrepreneurs, team members, support team, and mentors. In the professional category, there will be people you can choose and others you can't but the more you surround yourself with like-minded and value-driven people, the more fulfilling your days will be. Lastly, an important category for me is the personal development/growth category. In this category, the players often change quickly. It includes my business coaches, authors of books I'm reading, training courses, and podcasts. These are people I may or may not be interacting with, as in the case of a book I'm reading or podcast I'm listening to, but they are words and voices I intentionally choose to spend time with daily. This is a very important category that helps with growing to that next level.

Categories will change throughout your life. My parents, who are retired, may not have a professional category anymore, but instead have one for their volunteer groups they see daily. Thinking back to when I was a new mom, it was critically important for me to have other new moms in my circle because I was learning and wanted to follow others in the same boat. For someone who's dating and looking for a life partner, they might have groups that help towards the advancement of that goal. The groups will change and that's OK; what's important is consciously choosing which main players make up your groups because these are the people you will see on a daily, weekly, or monthly basis.

You may have noticed that one category I do not have is a peer or friend group. This isn't because I don't have friends or don't value what friendships bring to your life; quite the opposite, in fact. Friendships are extremely important and have a huge influence in one's life because friends give us a place to belong. As humans, we are made for community; our physical and mental health literally improves as we spend time with others and form strong bonds. Friends also play a significant role in shaping who we become and what we see as possible for our lives.

I didn't list a friend group because I am blessed to have friends in every single category. Friends are people who I enjoy spending time with and who love and support me. It's important to consider who your friends are and make sure their values align with yours. Even if you only see someone a few times each year, they will impact your life, and you want to make sure it's a positive one. Balancing these categories and the people who contribute to your life will lead to the greatest joy and fulfillment.

Free Friends and Paid Mentors—Expediting the Growth Journey

At the end of the day, who you surround yourself with has a tremendous impact on the quality and direction of your life. Some people we can choose such as a coach, mentor, or friends, and others we can't, such as bosses, family, or coworkers. The important thing to understand is that the key players surrounding you will have the greatest opportunity to influence you. Someone you see daily will have the capacity for greater influence simply due to the quantity of time in your life versus someone you see only monthly. We can't always choose these individuals, but when we're aware of their influence, we can make empowered decisions. We can simply accept the situation for what it is and focus our attention where it serves us.

If there are areas in your life in which the key players have a more negative than positive influence, you get to consciously decide how great their influence will be in your life. We all have people who get under our skin or rub us the wrong way. Sometimes the greatest opportunity for growth can come from these individuals and how we choose to respond to them, but in the end, you decide how much attention they deserve. What we focus on expands, so if their energy isn't serving you, choose to minimize your focus surrounding their energy.

On the flip side, anywhere that you can choose the key players, such as in personal development with a coach, in health with a positive personal trainer, or spiritually with an aligned peer group, you should deliberately choose to surround yourself with people who will raise you up and challenge you to be a better version of yourself. Look for people whose values and ethics are in alignment with your own, who choose a positive attitude and have ambitions to better themselves and those around them. The more people you have like this in your life, the less the negative individuals will affect you. Choosing the right people to surround ourselves with comes down to the value we place on our time and our self-worth. Time is more valuable than money because it's finite; we can't earn it or store it, and once it's gone it's gone. Who gets your time and attention should be one of the most important considerations in your day-to-day life.

There are two different ways to bring new people in your

life who can support you in getting to the next level: free or paid. Friends, colleagues, family, and other peer groups are typically free, meaning you're not paying for their time. One of the ways to expedite the growth journey and begin to surround yourself with the right people is simply by paying for them. Paid relationships can be coaches, trainers, mastermind groups, or any number of options. These individuals are tremendous assets to have in your corner when you're ready to grow.

Do You Need a Mentor, a Coach, or Both?

You've likely heard leaders talk about the value of finding a strong mentor, someone who can help coach and guide others in their professional journey through experience. Typically, this mentor will help answer career questions, provide guidance on decision-making, and be vested in a mentee's professional success. Mentorship can be a formal process whereby two individuals are matched at a company with an intended purpose of bringing up newer employees. Or it can be an informal process and more of a friendship and advice-seeking relationship. There's not a one-size-fits-all approach and it looks different for everyone. Very simply, it's one person helping another with the goal of creating a smoother path upward for the less-experienced individual. It can be a beautiful relationship that lasts years and can even turn into a deep friendship.

Mentorship is a great system and can be a wonderful asset, but many people get stuck wondering how to find someone to be their mentor as they advance in their careers. This is where coaches can be an addition to a mentor relationship. Investing in a professional coach is an investment in yourself. I have worked with a professional coach for almost half of the time I've been an entrepreneur. My coaches have changed over the years depending on where I am with my businesses or what level of coaching I need during each phase. The investment also increases each time I step into the next level of growth.

Coaching is typically a formal process. There are many career coaches out there that can be hired for a fee and follow a formal process. The biggest difference between a coach and a mentor is structure and financial exchange. A coach is someone you hire to help instruct you through a project, timeframe, or goal. There are coaches at all different financial levels and what you typically receive are a certain number of meetings, which can be over the phone, in person, or via video chat over a predetermined length of time. It might last a couple of months or a year and beyond. A coach is someone who hasn't necessarily walked the specific journey you're on so they're not going to give you answers to the challenges you're facing; their skill is in helping you identify the answers inside you through asking guiding questions. The goal of the coach is to help develop the individual, similar to a mentor but in a more formal process.

The biggest difference between a coach and a mentor, besides formality, is the fee structure. A mentor relationship typically doesn't have costs associated with it. In a coaching relationship, the level of investment increases with the coaches' experience and level of professional success. We're going to dive deeper into money and the value of investing in yourself in a later chapter, but for now, the important piece is that investment and perceived value go hand in hand in a coaching relationship. You're going to take coaching much more seriously and aim to reach the goals you set out to achieve when you're making an investment in yourself.

Why would someone need a coach? Professional coaching is not something readily discussed today. Many of us think we can get to the next level on our own and that it's a sign of weakness to ask for help or to hire someone to help us get there.

The truth is you can absolutely get to where you want to go on your own but hiring a coach will help you get there faster and easier. Don't get me wrong; advancing to the next level is never easy, but the road can be smoother with someone by your side navigating the twists and turns.

Many of today's well-known athletes work with coaches. In sports, it's a commonly accepted practice to work with a coach. It would be almost unthinkable to forgo coaching in any sport. A coach is an athlete's best ally. Coaches push them when they don't want to push themselves, know their limits and stretch them, help them keep the end goal in mind, and support and encourage them every step of the way.

A professional coach works in much the same way. They understand where you want to go, what your goals are, and they help you uncover what it's going to take to get there. Coaches are different than therapists and consultants. They don't give you the answers; they ask leading questions that help you discover the answers within you. The desires you have for your life are purposeful, they're not selfish, and they're the best thing for you. Working towards goals is a growth journey and the person you become in the process is the true reward. The resistance you feel when you're on the path and stretching yourself is exactly what you need to overcome and that's where a coach can help tremendously. A coach can help you stay on course and persevere. It won't be easy but it's more enjoyable when you have someone invested in your growth.

The fastest way to success happens by following someone who has come before you. Whether you have a mentor or you've hired a coach, be on the lookout for people you respect and admire who have had a similar journey. They may have a related career path or have worked through a challenge you're facing and can help you navigate your way through. There are always people a few steps ahead of you and behind you. The ones ahead can help you reach that next level and the one's behind could use a hand up. It's a beautiful cycle.

Business is Personal

I started my career prior to the introduction and widespread use of social media. Both at that time and early into social media's introduction, people looked at business and personal lives as two completely separate things. In fact, when social media began to spread, I remember having conversations with clients about whether they should have two social media profiles: one for work and one for personal. For the life of me, I could not understand the reason for that question or why in the world they thought it would be easier to manage not one but two separate profiles.

This is how many people thought about business—the person you were at work was somehow different than the person you were outside of work. In the end, I don't think many people decided to have two profiles, and the ones who did realized the wasted effort of maintaining both. No one wanted to be just a professional contact; it was an honor to be friends with the personal profile because, let's be real, if you're filtering your professional profile to the point that it takes out your personality, who wants that anyway? Thankfully—and I do believe it has been a blessing—social media now blurs the lines between one's professional and personal lives.

Many professional relationships eventually move to the online space where you can get to know someone better through seeing pictures of what they like to do on the weekends, photos of their family, and other aspects of their lives. This not only makes the relationship stronger, but more enjoyable. Let's face it: it's way more fun to do business with people we know, like, and trust.

I have always believed that business and personal are one and the same. The person we bring to work is the person we are outside of work. I understand that work demands more professionalism but if we're really walking the line of two different people inside and outside of work, it's only a matter of time before others catch on. Here's the deal: if you're really letting loose outside of work and doing some questionable things you wouldn't want your coworkers to see, don't put it online. In this case, it might be time to evaluate your decisions. Are you making the right choices outside of work to foster your growth? The same is true if you're only posting stale, professional, safe, or totally boring updates to your social media profile; you need to add personality because people will be attracted to who you are!

Choosing the people we work with is just as critical as choosing the people we surround ourselves with outside of work. We spend the majority of our days at work or on work priorities, so those we spend time with for work play an important role in our lives. In some cases, we can't choose who we work with, but when we can, it's important to consider the same aspects we would outside of work. Fortunately, as entrepreneurs, we have a lot of autonomy regarding who we work with. We are able to choose the people who support us through strategic partnerships as well as those who work for and with us.

In traditional business ownership, you're likely hiring employees, strategic partners, and clients. Don't make the mistake of hiring just anyone to fill these roles. The people who you spend the greatest amount of time with also have the greatest ability to influence how those days turn out, so make sure they are people who are deserving of your time. The biggest mistake new business owners make is devaluing themselves and what they have to offer. This leads to poor hiring decisions and ill-fitting client relationships. You do not need to take on every new business opportunity that comes your way, nor should you.

One example is in network marketing, where the goal is to build an organization of customers and other partners. To some extent, you get to choose those people. Imagine an organization with customers who constantly complain because they've never been happy with a purchase, even if they bought something at a 95% discount. Or business partners who never do the work but always want your time and attention to whine about why their business isn't growing. Now imagine an organization built on solid partnerships with others who are pursuing their dreams and excited about the future, and customers who are so grateful for the products you've introduced them to that they tell everyone and in turn, your business grows through referrals! The difference between these two businesses and what they add to your daily experience can make all the difference in whether you enjoy what you do.

Everyone would choose the thriving, energy-filled organization. But you might think, "I can't predict who will join me in business." As an entrepreneur, you can, and you do have control over who you pursue and who you allow to work with you. It's a shift in how you value yourself and your time and you don't have to take in everyone. We attract the level of leader we are becoming so if the only people coming into our lives choose to complain and see themselves as victims, there's only one place to look: in the mirror. The good news is when we look in the mirror, we are in control and we get to change. That's when it might be time to do some inner work.

Look, I get it; when you're a new business owner and just starting out, you're tempted to take every opportunity that

comes your way but don't make that mistake! Make sure
you think about every relationship and the long-term effects
before entering into any agreements. One similar situation
occurred with my first company when we were just starting
out. We heard talks that the largest company in our market
had expressed interest in working with us. At first, we were
thrilled! Our egos were doing a happy dance at the prospect of
landing the biggest fish in the pond; it made us feel like we had
made it. But as we started talking to other small companies like
ourselves that had worked with this particular company, we
heard all sorts of reasons why it might not be such a good idea.
In the end, we walked away from this major potential client
opportunity because it didn't fit the vision we were building in
our company. Our egos were bruised and we had to swallow
our pride, but it was the right decision for our long-term
growth. Take the time to evaluate whether each client is a good
fit for your culture. Working with someone who isn't will suck
your energy dry and prevent you from bringing that same "I'm
building a killer business" energy into the world that will attract
the right clients!

Hiring employees and creating strategic partnerships are
equally as important as choosing the right clients to work with.
When evaluating new business relationships, consider two
questions. First, is this person capable of doing the actual work
and qualified for the task? Secondly, would I want to spend
time with this person? The second question is just as important
as the first, but we rarely consider it because it doesn't feel like
a business decision. Somehow we get tangled up and think that
we need to choose the people we work with based on logic and
reason alone. Logic and reason are important components to
question number one, but the second question is critical. If
you don't enjoy working with someone, one or both of these
outcomes will result: you won't enjoy working with them,

which will cause you to avoid working with them, and/or you won't get the quality of output you desire.

Personal fit, that feeling you get when you interact with someone who's in alignment with you, is a really important metric to consider when growing your team. Consider the ability to choose who you work with as a tremendous blessing. You get to pick the kind of people who light you up, add to your excitement while building your dream business, and believe in you and your purpose.

In John Maxwell's Leadership Podcast, "E1: Winning is an Inside Job," he talks about specific qualities and characteristics to look for when picking leaders to follow and work with. These are the qualities and characteristics he looks for in the leaders he surrounds himself with and ones he recommends for others:

1. Commitment
2. Excellence
3. Integrity
4. Time Management
5. Attitude
6. Relationships
7. Priorities
8. Solid Family Values
9. Energy
10. Peace: A sense of deep peace

These are certainly characteristics we should consider when we're looking for coaches, mentors, or leaders to follow, but we should also consider these characteristics for those we work closely with in business.

Hiring Your Weaknesses Does Not Make You Weak

No one can do it all well. We all have strengths and weaknesses. There are tasks that light us up and there are those that don't. The key is admitting we can't do it all and setting ourselves and our businesses up for success by hiring our weaknesses. It took years and multiple businesses for me to finally admit that accounting, tracking expenses, or any task relating to tax planning and preparation made me cringe. I pretended to know what I was doing. I tried to handle all my business financials because that's what I thought a true entrepreneur did and I wanted people to see me as a competent business owner. My ego prevented me from asking for help. My husband finally blew the whistle after years of scrambling every tax season and trying to pull my financial documents together. We joked (through gritted teeth) every first quarter of the year that if our marriage made it past April 14th, we could make it through anything.

Eventually, through trying and continually failing, I hired someone to help manage the business financials. By the time I made this decision, it felt like a victory. I could spin my wheels doing something that drained my energy, or I could hire someone to help who is good at the financial piece and spend my time doing things that get me excited and add energy to my life.

Being an entrepreneur does not mean you have to do it all. That's one of the first traps many entrepreneurs fall into and it takes some time to retrain our brains into thinking differently. Just because it's yours does not mean you need to do it all. Doing it all is a surefire path to burnout and potential failure. Admitting you can't do it all takes courage and confidence. The idea that eventually flipped the switch for me was to ask myself, "Which tasks keep me up at night and which tasks get me up in the morning?" The tasks that get me up, jumping out of the bed and excited to take on the day are the ones that light me up and the ones I should be doing more of. The ones that cause me to lose sleep and feel stress and anxiety are the ones I need to outsource. Everyone has different "get up and keep me up" tasks. Some people love financials, God bless them, and when they are hired to do what they're good at, everyone benefits. Let people support you in doing what they love so that you can do what you love.

A hang-up for entrepreneurs is the idea of investing in help. In order to hire someone to support you, you need to pay them. Many entrepreneurs make the mistake of placing too much value on money conservation versus investment in the right areas. Saving money by doing everything yourself will cost you more in the long run. Time is money and your time is the biggest asset you have. It's okay to bootstrap the business but there are many online resources to find support people at a reasonable cost and less than what you should be charging for your time. Making smart hiring decisions can actually accelerate success and ensure things are done well.

Trapping Yourself

The Universe likes investment and boldness. When you have the courage to invest in others and hire your weaknesses, something magical happens; things seem to conspire in your favor. When we don't spend money and invest in hiring others to do the tasks we don't enjoy, we're really saying, "I don't believe enough in my dreams and this business to let money flow out." We're holding back and wherever there is hesitancy, negativity can squeeze through the cracks. When we instead make the bold decision to spend money, to believe that our business is worth the investment, good things happen.

You can feel this shift immediately, but it will also have a ripple effect afterwards. One of the blessings with this ripple effect is that when you decide to build a support team, it will become a group of people who believe in your vision and mission and can lift you up on days when you might doubt that vision. Your team will continue moving forward on their tasks and you will have no choice but to move forward on yours and that's the best thing to do when you feel stuck. Just putting one foot in front of the other is how you get unstuck and your team will help propel you in that direction. By building a team, you are essentially trapping yourself into success because these people are creating a swell with and around you towards your goals.

Determining who surrounds you and supports you in life and business is all about balance. It's balancing the people who will support your dreams and your growth and it's balancing where you need support. No one can do this alone and it's not weakness to admit you need others; it's strength. You will go further faster depending on who you have in your inner circle.

Journaling Prompts: Putting Pen to Paper and Getting Real

1. Let's get super honest about the people surrounding you right now. Do they support your dreams? Do they encourage you to grow? Do they challenge you to be a better version of yourself? Do they produce energy or drain energy?

2. Comparison is the thief of all joy. None of us is immune and thus, we need to be aware of when we're most susceptible. When do you most feel the comparison trap in your life? What activities produce comparison thinking?

3. We know that the people surrounding us have a profound impact on the quality of our life, but we don't often take the time to evaluate those key players. Take some time to evaluate the key players who make up your top categories and what changes need to be made.

   - Faith
   - Health
   - Professional
   - Personal Development
   - Community
   - Other

4. Are you willing to invest in your personal growth? Why or why not?

Taking the Lesson One Step Further with Recommended Reading

Mindset – The New Psychology of Success, by Carol S. Dweck, Ph.D.

We Saved You a Seat – Finding and Keeping Lasting Friendships, by Lisa-Jo Baker (Bible study)

One Action Step to Build Momentum

Have you thoughtfully considered all the areas of your business and personal life that could be outsourced? Really. Almost anything can be assigned to someone else which means if there are things, you're currently doing that drain your energy you can hire someone else to do them! It does not mean you're lazy, it means you're strategic, spending more time in areas that give you energy and fulfillment. First, write down everything you'd love to hand off and then visit my website, https://jessdennis.com/downloads for a helpful guide.

CHAPTER 5

Out of Balance—Losing the Keystone

"It's not because things are difficult that we don't dare, it's because we don't dare that things are difficult."
—Seneca (Roman philosopher, 1st century A.D.)

When Balance Became the Keystone

ARE YOU FAMILIAR with what a keystone is as it relates to architectural structure? When I studied abroad in Spain, we took many excursions to look at historic castles, bridges, and breathtaking buildings throughout the country. One of the structures we visited was a bridge that carried water from one part of the city to another. What was fascinating about this bridge in particular was that it wasn't assembled with any type of mortar or cement. It was formed by stones stacked so closely together that water could pass over them without falling through. The only way these stones could hold in their arch formation was through the use of a keystone. A keystone is a central stone at the summit of an arch, which locks the entire arch together. Without the keystone, everything falls apart. The keystone, while generally the same size as the other stones, plays a critical role in any arched structure.

Keep this visual in your mind because this is the role that balance has played in my life. The chapter you're about to read is what can happen when you lose this keystone. Balance is a nice idea and the thought of being a balanced entrepreneur sounds like it would be preferable to being an entrepreneur who's out of balance; a few years ago, I would have agreed with this cute idea. But as I will show you, I no longer look at balance as something that would be nice to have. Balance is now the keystone; without it, everything else falls apart. Just like the keystone of a structure, to an untrained eye it may appear as just another stone, but in the overall view of the arch, it's the piece that keeps all other stones in place, allowing the structure to function.

The Slippery Slope and the Drift

We've all turned on the news to see a headline about some politician or prominent business leader getting caught in a major scandal. We watch with our mouths agape, thinking, "How could they let this happen?" From the outside, they have everything most of us could only dream of achieving: the career, the success, the family, the fame, you name it; and they throw it away over something so careless, such an obvious mistake! We think, "Didn't they know that what they were doing was a terrible decision? How could they let this happen?" It happens because falling out of balance doesn't happen overnight and the results of being out of balance can be catastrophic. They didn't see that the small decisions were compounding to have massive consequences. They were just doing what they wanted in the moment, every day, through small decisions.

Imbalance happens ever so slowly. So slowly that sometimes we don't even see it happening and if we can't see it, most of the time others can't see it either until much later. It's that moment you look in the mirror, eyeing the extra twenty pounds you've put on and think, "When did this happen?" The truth is that it didn't happen in an instant. It happened every single day with each small decision over an extended period of time. It happens with the small bite here and there as you're feeding the kids, skipped days from the gym because it was raining, or you just didn't feel like going, or the idea that you'll start tomorrow, or next month when things slow down.

We can feel the drift—on some level we know it's there, but we don't pay it the attention it deserves. Why? Because today it's not affecting us. Today we're not dealing with the consequences because it's not that bad yet. But left untouched, these seemingly insignificant decisions can have massive consequences over time. In his book, *The Slight Edge*, Jeff Olson outlines this concept of simple disciplines or simple errors repeated over time and the results that ensue. The idea is that life is created in the moments, tiny moments, and thus, tiny decisions that seem inconsequential have massive results.

We can break down every area of our lives: finances, health, business, personal development, and relationships, and look at the actions or activities we take on a daily basis to either improve or neglect these areas. Typically, what is comfortable or easy to do now—skip the gym, watch television, shop online, scroll through social media, or skip the event—will become uncomfortable over time and lead to failure in key areas of your life. This is as opposed to doing what's uncomfortable now: hitting the gym, reading a personal development book, connecting with your spouse, or saving for retirement will become comfortable later because it leads to success. You're making decisions that either increase or decrease the value of your life, but you're never staying the same over time.

A Portrait of the Slippery Slope

Karen, a friend of mine, never struggled with her weight as a child or teen. In fact, she had been extremely active most of her life, playing high school sports and even competing in volleyball into her college years. She met her husband Steve while they were both attending university and had an immediate connection because he was extremely active as well and into outdoor recreation. On the weekends they would go hiking in the hills near campus or whitewater rafting.

After college they got married, moved back to Karen's small town where she had grown up, and each started their first jobs. The first few years were fun, an extension of their time in college. They were excited about entering their careers, buying their first home, and putting down roots. Eventually they talked about having children. They both loved children and knew they'd want a big family, so getting started early made sense. They had no trouble conceiving and were pregnant within a few months.

Karen loved being pregnant! She loved knowing she was growing a life inside of her and was determined to create the best atmosphere for that developing child. She stopped going to the gym because her doctor cautioned her about not getting her heartrate too high and she found it difficult to stay below the recommendation. She and Steve stopped going on hikes on weekends and most other outdoor activities for fear of Karen falling and what could happen to the baby. Most nights and weekends they stayed home, watching TV, and eventually getting the nursery ready.

Karen's doctor also cautioned her about weight gain during pregnancy. Of course, she was expected to put on weight but hers was getting higher than the "normal" zone they like to see for expectant mothers. Karen didn't worry about it though because she had always been fit and knew she'd get back to her previous life after the baby and lose the weight. After the baby arrived, Karen and Steve found themselves in entirely new roles as parents. They wanted to do everything by the book. They were swaddling, not letting the baby sleep on her stomach, feeding every couple of hours, nursing through the nights, and doing everything they could to tend to the new baby. Within a couple of weeks they were exhausted from the lack of sleep, frustrated, and stressed out. No one had told them honestly what this would be like. Still, they knew this was what they wanted, so they did their best.

Weeks passed, then months, and their beautiful baby girl was thriving. Eventually Karen went back to work. Every evening when work was through, Karen and Steve would rush home to spend time with their little girl. They no longer went out on date nights or hiked during the weekends because they each felt their lives had changed and spending time with their daughter was what they wanted to be doing. They spent most nights and weekends at home. Karen wasn't losing the weight as she had hoped. Nursing helped but that was now starting to decline. She thought she would get back to the gym but struggled to take time away from her daughter when she already felt that work took too much time from her.

As their daughter grew, they all settled into new routines as a family and it wasn't long before they were talking about having another baby. Karen got pregnant quickly again and their son was born the next year. This time, Karen had put on even more weight than the first pregnancy. She thought about the weight but assumed most women put on weight and eventually her life would slow down enough to lose it once the kids were older. For the next few years, Karen and Steve raised the kids while each moved up in their respective careers.

Their life wasn't perfect, but it looked like everyone else's they knew. All of their friends were in the same boat, so they never thought they should make changes. Karen's doctor had cautioned her about the state of her health; her back was in constant pain and affected not only how she felt during the day but was also keeping her up at night. She knew she needed to lose the weight but continually put it off, rationalizing that her kids needed her at home. She watched the scale climb every year, and with it additional aches and pains and health concerns. However, Steve eventually got back to what he loved and took up kayaking with a group of friends. Karen never came with him because she wanted to be with the kids.

Karen and Steve's story isn't unique. We see it happening to couples all around us. Their lives are out of balance and their values aren't in alignment with how they're living. Maybe you even find yourself in a similar situation. There are a couple of red flags and indications of where the Slight Edge is working against you. Karen's weight didn't become a problem overnight; it happened as life changed and over the span of years. Their marriage, once exciting and full of adventure, became stale as they discontinued date nights and stopped spending time together outdoors. This story doesn't need to continue for you to make assumptions about what could happen. Steve might connect with someone while he's spending time outdoors with his friends. Karen might continue to put on weight, growing more depressed and further from Steve. Any number of things are possible, but all are a result of the decisions they are making on a daily basis.

If we understand that imbalance happens over time as a result of our small decisions, why don't we all make better decisions? The first step is understanding how your decisions and actions can impact your life in the long-term so you're ahead of the game. The second key piece to understand is that while these decisions are simple, they're not easy. It's easier for Karen to sit at home with the kids instead of hitting the gym and rationalize it by saying that she's doing what's best for her family. It's easier for Steve to make new friends to go outdoors with instead of finding a babysitter and convincing Karen it's what's best for their marriage. We tend to make the easy decisions in the short-term, not what's best in the long-term. There are a handful of lies we tell ourselves in this process that contribute to the slippery slope, which we will discuss later in the chapter. Knowing what these lies are will help you identify them and put a stop to using them in your life.

My Story of Falling Out of Balance

After selling my first company, I had no plan. My plan had been to stay with the company and continue building for years, but that had all changed very quickly. I didn't know what would come next, so I stayed home with Wren while I contemplated my next move. I discovered for certain that I wasn't done being an entrepreneur, but I didn't know what my immediate next move would be. I had always envisioned starting another company, but as the months passed, I grew more and more anxious about that idea.

One day while at home with Wren, my phone rang from an unknown number.

"Hello, this is Jess," I said.

"Jess, this is Sydney Green with the Chamber of Commerce! How are you?" came the voice at the other end.

I had only met Sydney a short while before I sold my company, but we had become fast friends. I admired her immediately. She was this passionate, fiery redhead who was filling the shoes of a long history of male CEOs at our chamber. She was making waves in the community with her visionary ideas and new ways of doing business. She didn't fit the mold and that inspired me.

"Sydney! I'm doing great; how are you? It's so good to hear from you!" I said with both excitement and surprise.

"I'm running around like crazy but doing really well. How is life after selling and staying home with Wren?" she asked.

We caught up briefly about family and work. Then she said, "I want you to come work for me; what would it take?"

I drew in a sharp breath, trying not to give away my shock. I wasn't expecting this call and certainly wasn't expecting this conversation.

"Wow, I'm flattered," I replied. I felt reluctant about going back into employment after owning my own company, but I could feel that this was no accident. My gut instinct told me I needed to lean in and be open to this possibility.

"I would love to know what you have in mind," I said.

Sydney filled me in on the details and said she'd have her assistant get back in touch with me as soon as a job description was posted and the application process was open.

A month or so passed and when I received the application, I applied immediately and began the interview process. I was pleasantly surprised to feel at ease throughout the process. I enjoyed sitting across the table this time and being interviewed by others. Everything ran smoothly and after receiving the offer and working through a couple of negotiations, I accepted the position. I had a newfound appreciation for employment and was excited about this next adventure.

Getting My Feet Back Underneath Me

My new team was a wonderful mix of individuals from all different backgrounds, skillsets, and ages. They embraced me and I loved getting to know them. I enjoyed going to work just like I had prior to the recession. My role was meeting other business owners in our community, learning about their pain points and struggles in business, and connecting them with resources in our organization; it was a great fit with my background. I felt good; my co-workers appreciated me, and I wanted to do my best work. I was truly humbled and incredibly grateful to have the job.

Less than six months into my new role, we welcomed Emerson into our family on January 31, 2012. She was a big ol' happy baby. Unlike Wren, she slept well and was generally content unless she needed to eat, sleep, or be changed. I loved my time home with her and appreciated it in a different way the second time around. I actually followed the advice I hadn't the first time—I napped when she napped, I didn't think about work, and I allowed myself to stay in my PJs and relax without the pressure to be productive. It didn't hurt that it was the middle of winter and we were essentially snowed in throughout my maternity leave. My experience the second time around was much better and even though I was looking forward to getting back to work, I didn't feel the same internal pressure and guilt I had the first time. I was well aware of the potential for postpartum depression again so I did everything I could to support my mental wellbeing.

I took six weeks off, just as I had with Wren, and went back to work. As I was adjusting back to work and trying to fit into pre-pregnancy clothing, I started struggling with my weight. I had gained more in my second pregnancy and unlike the first, it didn't fall off while nursing. I was still carrying quite a few extra pounds when I returned to work and it made me uncomfortable. Because I had struggled so severely with postpartum depression after Wren, I wanted to do anything and everything I could to mitigate my chances of fighting that battle again. My physical being felt like a reflection of how I was feeling inside: uncomfortable, unsure, scared, and wanting to do anything to get back to who I was at my core.

I started working out as quickly as my doctor would allow. I was determined to lose the weight fast, so early morning workouts became my new addiction. The weight started to come off over time. Slowly but surely, I was seeing changes, but it took much longer the second time to lose the weight. I felt impatient. I wanted to see changes sooner but the fact that I was seeing changes at all kept me on track.

The Drift

Going back to work helped me feel like myself again as well. It felt purposeful and familiar. The team was excited to have me back and I was excited to be back. It didn't take long before I fell right back in step with where I had left off. The feelings I had experienced going back to work after having Wren were not present this time around. I had a better idea of what to expect and truthfully, it was easier being an employee and managing my time than when I had been an owner of a business. John and I felt like we were managing life as a family of four well, so as our work schedules started demanding more of us, we didn't feel the drift at first.

There wasn't one single moment in time but looking back, I can see how we were moving in different directions. John was fully in his role as president of his company. He had tremendous responsibilities on his shoulders and pressure to spend more time at work. After I had returned to work, I started falling into my old habits of attending many after-work events and spending less time with the family. John and I are wired for work, we love work, and we both enjoyed our careers immensely. While we knew we didn't want to miss this time with our girls, we never thought about what we needed to do to take care of our marriage. We took our marriage and relationship for granted, thinking it would just always stay strong.

I had heard of people prioritizing date nights but that was never a priority for us because we already felt busy enough with two young children and growing careers. I'm sure somewhere in the back of our minds, we figured we would focus on that when we had more time. That was a huge mistake.

Small Steps

In the spring, our office hired a new employee. He was younger and closer to my age than the rest of the employees. Most of our staff was older and more seasoned, so having someone from my generation who saw things from a similar perspective was a nice change. We became friends and at first, everything about our friendship was typical work colleague stuff. We'd catch up in the hallway or before meetings, chatting about typical office politics or the latest initiative. Our friendship was contained to work until I started attending more evening events.

The staff was close, so it wasn't unusual for our team to grab drinks downtown before one of our events. As I attended more events and went out with the team, my colleague and I started seeing more of each other outside of work. At first, we were surrounded by other team members because there was a whole crew, but over time the numbers dwindled until it was just us. We talked about all sorts of things and what started as a work friendship began to evolve. Our conversations became less and less about work and more about our personal lives. We got to know one another as people, as friends—where we grew up, where we went to school, our careers up to that point, what life was like outside of work, and what we did for fun.

I began to look forward to going to work and talking with my colleague. In the beginning, I should have noticed and paid more attention to the little red flags. There were glances across the room during meetings, longer conversations inside and outside of work, a new anticipation to go to work, and eventually, excitement to see him. One day over drinks I was the first to confess, "If the situation were different, I wonder if our friendship would be more?"

He smiled and said, "I've wondered the same thing." And with that confession it was clear that we both had feelings that were more than those of just friends.

My Confession

When John and I got married, we agreed that if either of us ever had feelings for someone else we would tell the other person right away, before acting on those feelings. I don't remember where this agreement came from or if we were just smart enough to know that you need to expose deceit as quickly as possible, but this pact was part of what would end up saving us. It was this commitment that pushed me to have the difficult conversation with John about my growing work relationship.

It was a Friday night after the kids had gone to bed and John and I sat down on the couch with a glass of wine and flipped on the TV.

"John," I half blurted out, forcing myself to initiate the conversation I had been dreading. "I have to tell you something."

John hadn't picked up on my awkwardness or the panicked

tone in my voice, so he half turned my way while flipping through channels. "What's up?"

"I have feelings for someone else" came tumbling out of my mouth. I was worried I would chicken out and not get the words out in the end, so unfortunately, I ended up blurting them out without the sensitivity they deserved.

He turned to look at me with confusion written all over his face and asked, "What do you mean?" I could tell his mind was reeling. He kept shaking his head and looking at me to try to understand what I was saying.

I explained what was going on at work and watched as his devastation set in. To be honest, I was surprised by his reaction, because my intention was to expose the feelings so that we could work through it together. I hadn't thought past this one conversation, which I'd hoped would change the course I was on. John was my best friend and I wanted to be honest with him and work through this with him. I was terribly confused about what I was feeling and why and I wanted his help. Looking back, I can see how short-sighted this was and how badly this conversation hurt John.

"Do you want to leave?" John asked.

"No! That's not what I want at all. I want to work on us, but I needed you to know," I said as my body grew flushed and my eyes darted around his face trying to understand what he was thinking. I couldn't believe he was asking that question. That's not what this was at all! I couldn't even believe I had developed feelings for someone else, but I needed John to know because I felt such tremendous guilt and shame. I knew our marriage was stressed and wanted to work on it; I had no intention of pursuing my feelings. I had an illusion of control over the situation.

We talked long into the evening, John asking questions as I tried to give the best answers I could. It was this conversation and my honest admission of how I was feeling that we both look back on today and believe was a huge part of the reason we came through it together.

The Storm

I wish I could tell you that after we had this conversation I woke up and realized I was dealing with fire and immediately changed my actions, but that would be a lie. My confession exposed the dangerous state of our marriage at the time. I am not one to pass off blame; the feelings I allowed myself to feel for someone else were entirely my responsibility, but the reality was we were not protecting our marriage like we should have. We simply didn't understand how important it was to prioritize a marriage if it's something you intend to keep. It's like anything else—you need to put energy in if you want energy out. We were both running in opposite directions and while we prioritized our kids, we didn't prioritize ourselves. We took our marriage for granted and made the mistake of assuming it would be fine without the attention it deserved. There were many nights and early mornings when we were just ships passing with no real conversation. We had no date nights or even uninterrupted moments together to connect briefly. We allowed life to get busy and made the dangerous assumption everything would be fine.

After my initial confession, John was heartbroken. His entire physical presence changed. The hurt behind his eyes was there every time he looked at me, his thoughts were somewhere else, and he drew away from me to protect himself. I had assumed that by being upfront and honest, the situation would be immediately restored, and we would grow back together, but the opposite occurred. Our distance grew further by the day, making life at home very uncomfortable.

Work is where I chose to escape. I thought that because my colleague and I had admitted our feelings, we would cut ties, but that's not what happened. I spent more time at the office and with my colleague. We started exploring what this all meant, dissecting our feelings. If I could go back in time and change anything, it would be this. It's not unusual to feel attracted to someone else, but once the feelings were out in the open, we should have immediately stopped talking. Instead, we spent more time talking together. Because I had assumed this would never happen to me, I started to wonder if this was happening for a reason, and my cracks of doubt started to spread.

I began to believe the lie that my life could be different, maybe better with someone else. My colleague wasn't married and he didn't have a family, so on the surface his life seemed uncomplicated and untethered. This caused me to reflect on what my life was like back before kids, when I could live for myself and do what I wanted. I began to resent my situation and all of my responsibilities. I began to resent how hard our lives had become at home. John and I had spent over a decade together at that point, so I remembered well what life was like before kids, before demanding careers and before things had grown stale, and I mourned that life we loved together. John was feeling depressed and instead of working through that with him, I chose escape and turned to my growing feelings for someone else.

One evening I told John I was going out with friends and wouldn't be home until late. I told him not to wait up for me and that I'd see him in the morning. I lied. I didn't go out with friends; I went out with my colleague. We spent hours talking over cocktails about everything from work to life and eventually, what life might look like if we pursued our feelings. I was wrapped up in the fantasy of what life could look like with someone else in an entirely different situation. I believed the lies and desired another life.

I went home in the wee hours of the morning. As my head hit the pillow, my mind was spinning with a million questions. The next morning, I awoke to John holding my phone, staring at the screen, his face twisted between devastation and fury. My head was pounding from the cocktails the night before, but I forced myself awake because I knew something was wrong.

"Who were you with last night?" he asked through gritted teeth.

I sat up, fighting my way through the fog. I said nothing, and he dropped the phone on the bed and walked out. I picked up my phone and saw a text message from my colleague. The message made it perfectly clear that we had been hanging out because it was an extension of our conversation the night prior.

John left that day. He walked out and I thought he wasn't coming back. I will never forget the moment he left. I was sitting at the top of our stairs, Emerson still sleeping in her crib and Wren playing down the hall in her bedroom. I listened to Wren's tiny voice playing with her toys as John walked out and the door slammed shut. His heart was shattered, and it was all my fault. I had allowed someone else to enter my heart and as a result, I had completely broken the one who loved me most. In an instant, all the trust that had taken years to build was gone as John walked out the door. I felt desperately alone, with two kids and only myself to blame.

I don't know why it took that moment, but in an instant the question became unquestionably clear of what I wanted for my future. I stood up, walked away from the stairs and back into our bedroom, pulled out a notebook from the nightstand along with the pen and started writing. By some miracle, Wren kept herself entertained while I wrote for what seemed like hours. When I was done, I had pages and pages lying in front of me.

Pages written for John detailing everything from my dreams for our future, to where I thought we went wrong, my mistakes and how I would give anything to make things right. I didn't know if he would come back and if I'd have the opportunity to give him the letter, but I knew if we tried to have the conversation out loud, I wouldn't be able to tell him everything I was feeling.

Despite the pain of that moment, I can now look back and say that what I experienced sitting on the stairs that day was a tremendous blessing. I knew, beyond a shadow of a doubt, that I was meant to be with John. His leaving jolted me into reality and where we were headed. How had I let this happen?

He came back later that day. Thankfully, he had confided in his dad who told him to come back and talk before making any drastic decisions. The minute he walked through the door I met him with tremendous repentance. He didn't want to talk to me and made it perfectly clear that he didn't know if he wanted to be with me, but that he'd come back because he wasn't sure if he wanted to leave either. I handed my letter to him and just asked that he read it. I apologized and gave him the space he needed and desired.

That day, we started the path back to completeness. It would take years to restore what we had, but we have built it even stronger, beginning the journey that day.

The Fine Print

I didn't include a lot of the details of my story, which most would be curious to know. But I didn't include them for several reasons. First and foremost, it's private. I'm a pretty open book but my story doesn't just impact me; there were many people involved, most importantly John and the girls. And while I wouldn't mind sharing the details, I know they might not feel the same way. The colleague is out of my life entirely and unaware of this book, which is also why I wrote the story leaving out the details—to protect his privacy.

But the biggest reason I left out the details is because they simply don't matter. Almost every woman I know has a story of some sort of betrayal, infidelity, or an affair. Every story is different, and every person defines it differently. While the details might make for a more riveting read, they aren't what matter. If I gave you the details of my story, I can guarantee you'd be disappointed. My story wouldn't be categorized as a typical affair. In fact, when writing this chapter, I first called it "infidelity" and even that word felt too strong for John and me. Betrayal felt more accurate. But no matter what it was or how we define it, it was just as damaging as a full-blown affair.

The situation I found myself in was the result of living an imbalanced life. I was leaning too far into work while simultaneously neglecting my marriage. I was focusing on my health and trying to get back in shape, but it was at the cost of my relationships. My priorities were off and when our priorities are off, even small daily steps in the wrong direction can have massive consequences.

In a book about entrepreneurship, why did I include this story? It wasn't because I wanted to expose myself for the mistakes I've made. Most people in my life don't even know about this painful time in my past, including many family members. For most people in my life, reading this book will be the first time they learn about the betrayal. John and I worked through this privately with a handful of our closest friends and a few family members. We chose to work through it that way because we were embarrassed. I thought I was the only person I knew who'd screwed up like this and it felt like a mistake that would define me for the rest of my life. I know that sounds extreme, but when you're in the middle of a mess it can be hard to see it for what it is. Beginning to talk about what happened and sharing my mistakes with others is what started the healing process. The more I've opened up and in writing this book, I'm beginning to learn that infidelity on all sorts of levels affects just about every couple I know personally. You read that right, almost every single couple I know has a story. I want to be as straightforward as possible here, because it's important. It is my passion and purpose to encourage women to pursue entrepreneurship, which will likely take them out of the home to some extent and interacting with more male counterparts. I believe that discussion around and awareness of this topic go hand in hand. Having more women in entrepreneurial roles will have an impact on their individual families. Look, entrepreneurship and business leadership are still positions primarily held by men. Most businesses are run by men. As we see more and more women stepping into these leadership positions and starting businesses, the dynamics will start to shift. My goal in sharing my experience and what I've learned from talking with fellow female entrepreneurs is to expose this dangerous potential pitfall of success: when you're doing what sets your soul on fire and living your purpose, you're one hot momma! Anyone who's excited about what they're doing and taking on each day with a zest for life will attract all sorts of attention, most of it good and helpful but not all of it. Attracting others is a good thing, so long as you know what to watch for when it's attracting something that's not serving you or your mission.

The biggest thing that held me back when walking through this very dark time in my past was the secrecy. I didn't talk to anyone for a very long time about what we were facing as a couple and that was the wrong decision. The healing process began the minute we exposed it to those who loved us, supported us, and wanted us to work through it as a couple. For those women who never face this devastating situation, I am happy for you.

For those who find themselves in a similar situation, I pray this chapter changes the outcome of your present reality, how you talk to your partner, and how you open up with others.

If the small decisions we're making every single day can have such a profound impact on our lives, why doesn't everyone choose to make the right decisions? Again, doing what's best for us is typically the very thing we don't want to do. I've heard other leaders say that if you want to change your life and you're not sure where to start, just start doing all the things you don't want to do. It's how we're wired—we don't want to eat the salad, we want the cheeseburger, and we'd rather watch TV on our couch while snacking on potato chips instead of hitting up the yoga class. You'll hear me say this a lot, but it's human nature. We lean in to what feels good now and we'll sacrifice what's good for us in the long run every single time. It's important to understand this concept if you're going to change your life and make smart decisions now. Your brain won't like it and it'll be yelling at you to stop and do what's easy the whole time, but you know what's best for you, so you make the difficult decisions anyway.

Believing the Lies that Lead to Imbalance

Lie #1: It's Fine

"How are you?"

"I'm fine, thanks." This has become the standard response. We respond so easily, without any thought, because we *are* fine. Aren't we? We don't have any major complaints and things are going fairly well. We could certainly have it worse and even though things could be better, it's fine. So, what's wrong with fine? In the book, *Stop Saying You're Fine* by Mel Robbins, being fine is defined as "blah" and keeps you stuck. If your brain can convince you you're fine, there's no need to fix anything. Fine is fine if it's allowed.

"When it comes to the areas of your life that are blah, bothering you, or broken, your brain does three clever things: it convinces you that you are fine even though you feel blah; it keeps you so busy that you have no time to stop and think about what's truly bothering you; and it focuses your attention on the surface-level, easy stuff that you feel comfortable talking about so you can ignore what's broken." (pg. 107)

The problem is that "fine" has become the default and when it's a default, we don't stop to consider its repercussions. Fine is a little lie we tell ourselves and others that allows the truth to remain hidden. If we actually stopped and considered how we're really doing in the most important areas of our lives, it would be hard to say we're fine. Take marriage, for example. We say it's fine as we shrug our shoulders even though we haven't had a date night in years, we barely talk to our partners, we run around daily, and don't even get me started on sex! It's not fine. If just for a moment we stopped to consider what would truly make us happy and what we had imagined when we took our vows, we would make some serious changes. It becomes fine when we give up, when we believe this is how it's supposed to be, or we observe the same pattern with others in our lives. It all starts with identifying the lie and believing it can be different.

The Truth: Put Equal Work Into the Areas That Matter Most

While living through my betrayal, it occurred to me that as I was working so hard to achieve career success, I hadn't stopped to consider what family success would look like. Just like what we discussed in Chapter 3, the plan for your life is actually more important than the plan for your business. But few of us take the time to consider that plan. Deciding how you want your life to look is essential, with business and career being part of that plan, but they're not the *entire* plan. I made the dangerous assumption that my marriage and family would be just fine while I focused on my career. That I didn't need to put work into my marriage, that John and I would have a strong relationship, and things would only get better for us the more successful we became. Wrong! This could not have been further from the truth and this "it's fine" lie was the very first one I believed. Energy in equals energy out. Some people don't like to think of their relationships as work, and if that's the case for you, think of it as energy. If you don't put energy into the relationship, you won't get a whole lot of energy out.

The day John walked out, it hit me—if I didn't start prioritizing family and marital success like I was with my career, I was going to find myself alone. Continue on the same path and I would end up financially successful but without the people who mattered most. That was a sobering wakeup call. Most of us measure success as financial on some level, and there's nothing wrong with pursuing financial success so long as it's in check with everything else. If you have a family or partner and intend to keep those people in your life when you're raking in the dough, then you'd better prioritize them now.

What does prioritization look like? If you're like me and thinking about business comes more naturally, think about how you prioritize your business. You spend time on it daily. You have goals and plans for moving forward in the years to come. The exact same is true for marriage and family. Spend intentional, uninterrupted time daily with those you love. Enjoy cell phone-free meals together while having actual conversations. Be intentional and focused. Make plans for what you want to see and do as a family. What trips do you want to take in the next twelve months or five years? Are there sites you've never been to in your own backyard that you can prioritize?

For your marriage, plan date nights and fun things to do on the regular. So many of us fall out of dating our spouse and then wonder why the magic is gone. Well, duh! We aren't doing any of the same things we did in the beginning to get them! Think like you're a couple dating, before marriage and kids. What did you do for and with your partner? Don't overthink it; just do what makes you happy. You'll know when you're getting it right. You'll feel it.

Lie #2: That's Not Me.

One of the other traps I unknowingly fell into was the "I would never do that; that's not me" trap. I didn't even know this was a trap until I started talking to others and learning about couples who had also dealt with betrayal and infidelity. This particular lie isn't one of superiority or delusion; it's truly just not understanding that humans are human and we all make mistakes. The very thing that makes us human and allows us to find a life partner and desire to start a family is the very thing that can cause us to question if we married the right person or started a family too soon. Desire is a part of life, no matter how you were raised, how faithful you are, how many times a week you attend church, or how committed you are to your spouse. Many who find themselves in this situation were not looking for it and if you would have asked them if this could ever happen to them, they would have answered "no" without taking a breath, blinking an eye, or hesitating for a second.

This thought process is very similar to that of cancer or other catastrophic health concerns. We know it's out there, we know it happens to other people, but we never imagine it will happen to us. Fortunately for us, unlike cancer, knowing the necessary signs and taking the appropriate precautions can prevent imbalance from occurring in your life. Knowing that others feel the same way you do—that it could never happen to them—is important when this little lie creeps up. This lie tricks us into putting ourselves into potentially dangerous situations. If we believe it could never happen to us, we miss the red flags. For example, when we received that super kind compliment from that really nice guy and now we can't get it out of our heads. Instead of alerting our precautionary response, it endears us to him and we might find ourselves spending more and more time with him.

My friend Karen told herself this same lie. Because she had lived her entire life up until family and having children as an active person, she had no reason to believe she'd be anything different than active afterwards. But as we saw in her example, the creep happens, and the slippery slope is quite slippery. One skipped day at the gym leads to another and another. If instead Karen had understood that life happens to everyone and even the most active people can become sedentary through life's changes, she might have seen herself and her health as a greater priority. When we stop believing we're immune or invincible, we can see ourselves and our weaknesses for what they are and create a plan.

Lie #3: I'm Not Doing Anything Wrong.

This lie is all in the details and how we justify our actions. The drift happens ever so slowly so that when we view our actions individually, they seem inconsequential. Skipping a day at the gym because we're not feeling it is justifiable—no one has perfect days and we all need rest, right? Here's where things can get a little tricky, because it is true that rest is important and a necessary piece of living. But it can also be an excuse, a rationalization, and no one will know but you. For the "I'm not doing anything wrong" lie, we need to police ourselves. We're often the only ones who can identify the truth from the lie.

This is an especially important lie when it comes to betrayal. Most people in this situation never in a million years thought they'd be dealing with this and are actually confused as to how they got there. You might be reading this and thinking, "How in the world can someone betray their spouse and have no idea how they screwed up?" This is why this is a critical lie to understand. Betrayal often starts with decisions that seem benign. Unlike what the movies would like us to believe, it's usually not a steamy decision made one night in the bar after many stiff cocktails. No, for most, it's teeny tiny steps away from our partners and closer to someone else. Steps so small that only you can identify them by how they make you feel and it's in the feeling that the lie is exposed. The steps are different for everyone but can include: more time with someone else rather than your partner, even if it's for work purposes; a compliment that lingers in your mind too long; taking a little extra time to get ready to look good for others; weight loss for the wrong reasons; a glance; a smile; sharing innocent but private information with someone else; a Facebook message or text; or any number of things that appear innocent on the surface but feel off internally.

The most challenging part of this lie is that we don't want to do what we need to do, so we turn to the lie because it lets us off the hook. Doing what's right often doesn't feel good while we're doing it. Skipping the gym, eating the cake, paying more attention to your coworker than your spouse all feel better than doing the hard work, doing what you know needs to be done. Again, you know what you need to do, you know what's right, you just have to discipline yourself to do it.

Lie #4: I Can't Recover From This.

Out of all the lies, this one hits me the hardest and makes me the saddest. This is the lie we tell ourselves after the damage has been done. It keeps us stuck and often brings us deeper into shame and regret. This lie tells us that no one else has been where we are, and no one has screwed up as badly as we have. When we believe this lie, we pull inward. We don't talk to others, we live in secrecy, and we don't take the steps necessary to get out of the mess we've made. It could be 50, 100 or 200 pounds overweight and we think, "How did I get to this point? There's no turning back now. No one else I know is in this situation; no one will understand."

This lie typically happens once we can no longer believe the other lies. We've admitted to ourselves that we're not fine, that this can happen and has happened to us, and that we've definitely made some wrong decisions. All the other lies got us to this point and the intention of this lie is to keep us in this situation. It takes tremendous courage to admit we've screwed up and we need help. We fear judgment from others because from our vantage point, we can't see that others have dealt with their own messes. But I've learned something so beautiful about mistakes and admitting our shortcomings: We've all made them, and we all have them. The fact that you're in this situation makes you human and relatable to others.

I was surprised people didn't abandon me when I admitted my betrayal. My spouse didn't abandon me. My friends didn't abandon me. I was remorseful and I wanted to fix the mess I had made, but I needed help and part of that healing was telling others. Living in secrecy and shame was keeping me stuck, keeping me imbalanced. This wasn't something I could fix on my own; I needed others. But first I had to be OK with admitting my faults to myself. Look, I'm not saying it's easy; it was the hardest thing I've ever done. But I wouldn't be where I'm at if I hadn't shut down this last lie.

PSA: Here's my plea that you understand the consequences of this lie. Believing we cannot recover from the mistakes we've made is a very dangerous lie and ensures that we stay out of balance. We all make mistakes; we all have periods when we lose our keystone of balance. I don't care how bad you think your situation is or if you don't think anyone else has done what you've done. You can absolutely recover from any level of imbalance. Believing this lie can be a life or death matter and it is my mission to expose it and help others. I know the darkness and deep pain from believing this lie and I want to help others find the resolution and peace that can come from taking steps out of this place. If you're in a place where you have pain that you need to work through, I want you to take the first step. Talk to a loved one, a friend, a family member or pastor, talk to someone else and allow them to walk with you through to the other side.

Journaling Prompts: Putting Pen to Paper and Getting Real

1. Through my story and Karen's, we explored how seemingly insignificant daily actions compound over time to shape the direction of your life. John Maxwell says, "You will never change your life until you change something you do daily. The secret to your success if found in your daily routine." What is your daily routine? Are you doing something daily that contributes to growth in your most critical areas?

Taking the Lesson One Step Further with Recommended Reading

The Slight Edge, by Jeff Olson

One Action Step to Build Momentum

This was a heavy chapter. My story illustrates what can happen when we've fallen out of balance. Often, we don't immediately notice the fall. It's usually after we're in a mess that we wonder how we got there and how to get out. A mess looks different for everyone, too; it can be health, faith, marriage, relationships, work or any number of things. If you're in a mess right now I want you to take the first step and talk to someone. You will not feel like it and you'll be worried about what they'll think of you because you're likely disappointed in yourself but talking to someone else and asking for help is the fastest way back on track. If you're not in a mess but want to stay on track, I want you to think of one key area in your life that could use consistent attention. Maybe it's your marriage and you want to implement date nights. Maybe it's your health and you want to create better habits to take care of yourself. Whatever it is, think of one area and one activity that you can do daily to strengthen that area of your life and do it now.

CHAPTER 6

Money: It's Not Dirty to be Ambitious

"I bargained with Life for a penny,
And Life would pay no more,
However I begged at evening
When I counted my scanty store;
For Life is just an employer,
He gives you what you ask,
But once you have set the wages,
Why, you must bear the task.
I worked for a menial's hire,
Only to learn, dismayed,
That any wage I had asked of Life,
Life would have paid."

— Jessie B. Rittenhouse

My Million-Dollar Goal

I'VE FOLLOWED MANY whims in my life, and the million-dollar goal started as just that: a whim. For me, a whim is an idea you have in a moment that captures your attention.

Something you think about that doesn't have to be profound but sticks with you. It can, and normally does feel crazy and scary to say out loud, but something about it feels purposeful and authentically you. We talked about this idea back in Chapter 2 with belief and listening to your inner voice; a whim is a similar idea. It's your inner voice or higher power connecting with you and leading you in the direction of your purpose.

I wouldn't have started, purchased, sold, and built businesses, or be sitting here writing this book without my million-dollar whim. It happened when I was twenty-five years old, shortly after I started my first company. I don't remember the exact moment but at some point, it hit me that I wanted to make a million dollars by the time I was thirty years old. Maybe a better way of saying this is that it hit me and then continued to hit me. The first time it happened, I brushed it off, because it wasn't really a profound idea, and who doesn't want to make a million dollars? I was probably thinking this was just another hare-brained idea that had come to mind and wasn't worth pursuing. But it continued to come back, over and over until it eventually caught the attention it deserved. It finally stopped me and when I gave serious consideration to how one would make a million dollars, I didn't have the answer. I presumed there were many ways but I couldn't answer that for myself. My curiosity took over, which it often does, and I set out to find an answer.

At first, I was quiet about my million-dollar dream. It felt crazy and yet laughably commonplace at the same time. Was I was aiming too high or was I silly and aiming too low? It made me feel childish, like saying I wanted to be the president of the United States. Doesn't everyone want to make a million dollars? What's so profound about this idea? It felt simple and ridiculous, and yet I had no idea how I was going to achieve it. Deep down I knew I was capable, but I didn't have a plan, nor did I know anyone else personally who had a similar goal or a path to get there. Looking back, I can see that the seeds of the million-dollar goal began to lay the foundation for eventually exiting the business I owned at the time, my first business. I needed to surround myself with other million-dollar dreamers because they weren't in my circle yet.

I come from a hard-working Wisconsin family. My parents both worked and did well for us. We grew up in a beautiful, baby blue Colonial home surrounded by thick forest, on a golf course where I spent my childhood selling golf balls back to golfers who would lose them in the woods. Eventually my parents purchased a second home in Northern Wisconsin—a cabin on a moderately-sized fishing lake three hours north of our home to get away on weekends as a family. Although there were certainly things we wanted and didn't have, we always had more than enough and were afforded many memorable experiences through annual family trips to Mexico or other parts of the U.S.

My parents instilled a strong work ethic in us through the delegation of household chores and conversations around the dinner table about the privilege to work and earn money. My sister, brother, and I were expected to help out around the house, anything from general cleanup to chopping and stacking wood for the fireplaces. In exchange for chores, we earned a weekly allowance to save if we chose or spend on lunches out with friends during the school week.

My parents were savers. Both of them had humble upbringings. When my dad was growing up, his father passed away and he was raised by a single mom who never remarried. She raised him and his brother in a small home and provided for them through nursing. Throughout my childhood, I heard many stories about his upbringing and how little they had. My dad owned only two shirts and one pair of pants that he washed and ironed daily so he wouldn't get made fun of any more than he already did by kids at school.

My dad never forgot his roots and was grateful for what he had made of himself and for his family. He made sure we understood how fortunate we were by telling us stories of what it was like for him growing up. His stories helped me understand the privileges we so easily took for granted, things like two living parents who both had jobs with income and even our health, things that are easy for anyone to take for granted, but especially children who know no other way. By comparison, we had an abundance of blessings, financial and otherwise, and there was a part of me caught between gratitude and desiring more for my life.

I think most parents want more for their kids than what they are able to provide for them, but as a child, we're afraid of wanting more than what our parents provided. It felt selfish or ungrateful to want more because we always had more than enough. I wanted to appreciate all we had and yet I knew from an early age that I was meant for big things.

Eventually, I shared my million-dollar goal with John. His response was straightforward. He simply said, "Cool," and then asked, "Is that a million dollars in the bank, a million dollars after tax earnings, or a million dollars net worth?"

His questions puzzled me; I hadn't considered those things. To me, the goal was straightforward: a million dollars by 30. I wasn't clear on what it would look like or how I would know when I achieved it, but deep down, I also felt I wasn't meant to know the details. I was simply meant to focus on the million dollars.

After telling John, I sat with my goal, turned it over in my mind, and started sharing it with others. The responses were eye-opening and entirely varied. In general, men didn't really get it and often asked me clarifying questions like John had, but were never shocked by the goal. Women, on the other hand, had a much different and far more fascinating response. Women didn't care for the goal. Actually, not only did they not care for it, they straight-up rejected the goal. Instead of asking questions after I shared it, they would size me up, usually squinting their eyes as they looked at me, pursing their lips, and not saying anything at all. If they made any sound, it usually came from the back of their throats and sounded more like a short "hm," and that was it. Long after the conversation had passed, if you can even call it that, I'd hear through the grapevine that the woman I'd told had said to someone else that I was selfish, greedy, money-hungry, and only cared about myself. Of course, they never said these things to me directly, but I knew it was a result of sharing my goal with them.

Of course, hearing that people were saying these things about me hurt. It wasn't the truth at all, and I thought they all knew me better than that. But something in their reactions also piqued my curiosity. I had expected other women to be excited and talk about how to make this a reality for themselves as well. I had hoped to find other women who wanted the same thing and to have someone else to strategize with and dream. I couldn't understand why all women didn't have this goal for themselves. The dream I thought would sound silly was actually offensive to many! This was an eye-opening realization and once I determined I couldn't talk with other women about it, I did what I always do when I need to find answers. I turned to books.

I started reading any and all books I could get my hands on pertaining to making money. I read *Millionaire by Thirty* (there is such a book, believe it or not) by Douglas R. Andrew, *Think and Grow Rich* by Napoleon Hill, *The Difference* by Jean Chatzky, *How Successful People Think* by John C. Maxwell, *Secrets of Six-Figure Women* by Barbara Stanny, and many more that line my bookshelf to this day. These books expanded my belief in what was possible, opened my mind up to new opportunities, and exposed me to people and ideas that would allow this dream to become a reality.

I started to believe my goal was purposeful. I looked at business earning opportunities, but I also looked outside of business. At one point, I even contemplated applying for *The Amazing Race* because winners receive a million dollars, but in the end I didn't because I couldn't figure out who my partner would be. One thing was for certain, it was a clear goal and I wanted to solve the puzzle. The questions John had posed made sense but felt unnecessarily complicated. I knew the goal was a million, period. No before or after taxes, no complicated formulas or equations, just a million.

Years passed and as my thirtieth birthday approached, I still hadn't hit my goal. John encouraged me to add up my lifetime earnings to see where I was, but something didn't feel right about that. It wasn't meant to be complicated; I wasn't supposed to add anything or spend my time trying to figure it out, it was simply a million. Instead of feeling discouraged about not reaching my goal, I decided that if I turned 30 and still hadn't reached the goal, I would extend it by five years. I'd set the new goal of a million by 35. It didn't quite have the same ring, but it felt right. I knew I needed to stay laser focused on this goal because, again, it was purposeful.

The year I turned 30, I received an unusual message from a woman who held an impressive position with a prominent business in Wisconsin. She asked if we could connect because she was expanding her network marketing business in the area. This was during the time I was working at the chamber of commerce and looking for a new business opportunity. So of course, when I received her message, I responded that we should absolutely connect! We got on the phone and she shared about her business with me. During the course of our conversation, she told me it would be possible for someone to make a million dollars in five years with this business.

That was all I needed to hear. I didn't know this woman; I didn't fully understand the business yet, but my decision was clear. This was the path I was meant to follow. I joined her in business a week later and spent the next few years learning on my feet while working and growing my own network marketing business. Along with learning everything I could about the business and doing my best to build quickly, I made personal development my new addiction and never stopped growing.

During my sixth year in business, I turned 35 years-old. One Saturday morning, I was sitting in my bed, laptop in my lap, getting a few things done before the girls woke up. I had started the day slowly, with a cup of coffee, and decided to check in on business from bed. I'm not sure why it hadn't occurred to me until then to check my numbers. I had known it was coming, but I had spaced and didn't think to check until this moment. I logged into the system, opened up my dashboard where I could see the state of my business, and there it was. It was clear as day and didn't take an accountant, a calculator, or any fancy equations. I simply saw a one followed by six zeros and some change: $1,000,000. I didn't have to add any numbers or track lifetime earnings; I saw it right there on my computer.

I'll never forget the feeling I had as I looked at the numbers on the screen. I had always imagined this being exhilarating, exciting, and a moment when I'd jump up and down screaming with glee. But that's not what it was like at all. It was this deep down calm, a peacefulness. I saw and experienced firsthand what it felt like to see a dream realized. I had worked on this goal for ten years and I knew it was coming, so seeing the numbers was no surprise. It wasn't the excitement I'd imagined because it wasn't shocking; it wasn't like winning the lottery and the people you see on TV hugging their family members and crying. This didn't happen in a moment, it happened over years and years of hard work and personal development.

I smiled to myself, looked out the window, and tried to sit in the moment to truly appreciate the accomplishment. The house was quiet; John was making a cup of coffee in the kitchen and as I looked out the window, a flock of geese flew by in their "V" formation. This was it; I had made a million dollars. I called John in and shared with him that I officially hit the goal and showed him the numbers on my screen. He smiled and said, "Way to go" as he stuck out his closed hand to give me a fist bump. In bed, wearing PJs, over a cup of coffee, we exchanged a million-dollar fist bump. That was the celebration.

That day, as I reflected on the journey, it all made sense. The million-dollar goal was never about the money; it was about the journey, the growth, the people, and the opportunities. That million dollars represented who I had become in my ten-year quest. It took twice as long as I had thought it would, and I couldn't have predicted the path or the outcome. The million-dollar Jess was an entirely different person than the one who had set the goal. I learned a very important lesson through that journey: You earn what you become. My 25-year-old self wasn't a million-dollar earner, but my 35-year-old self was. I had earned a million dollars because I had grown into the person who was worth a million dollars.

Men, Women, and Why We Differ on Money

When I set my million-dollar goal, I assumed everyone would be on board. I actually assumed it was silly to set this goal because I thought everyone else was already working on *their* million-dollar goal. I thought I was late to the party. But boy was I wrong! When I started sharing my goal, it wasn't because

I wanted to brag, it was actually to find my people that wanted the same thing, so we could help one another get there. I was shocked to not find a soul! Men snickered at the simplicity of it and women turned their noses up. I can honestly tell you I was confused by these reactions and this is what drove me to explore this idea further. I couldn't understand what was happening based on my assumptions of how I thought people would react. Since hitting the goal, I have found one or two women who've had the same goal and when I've asked them about reactions from others, they've reported similar experiences.

None of this is meant to bash women in particular. I believe women have the hardest time with money because they come at it from a heart position. We make money personal because it IS personal. What we could do with money could change the world and we can feel that energy deep down inside.

Where do all these beliefs come from? Why wouldn't everyone have this goal and why are women in particular so put off by this goal? Money itself is not bad. Money is money; it's a means of exchange. It's simply a way we put a value and price on the goods and services in our lives. We *assign* all of the meaning to it. The stories we've created or taken on about money have nothing to do with actual money. This is where we need to get super clear and break up with our stories.

Your Beliefs Become Your Reality

How did you feel when you started reading this chapter knowing we were going to talk about money? What was your reaction when I said I wanted to make a million dollars? What if I used the word rich? Would you prefer well-to-do or financially stable over rich? It is very important for us to consistently check our thoughts and physical reactions to words, phrases, beliefs, and conversations about money. Our past, stories we've learned, or stories we've created for ourselves have a huge impact on whether we bring money into our lives or not.

You cannot become that which you despise or bring into your life anything you knowingly or unknowingly reject. The truth is many of us aren't paid what we're worth because we've made money complicated and ugly. If you're not super clear on your beliefs and feelings around money, that's the first step. If you desire to make more money, we need to get to the bottom of how you feel about money.

The reason money is emotional is because we've all had those experiences with or without money that have defined our thoughts and feelings about it. Most of the negative stories we hold are from times we lacked financial control. The stories are often fear-based and hard to release. As humans, we're meaning makers so we're constantly trying to make sense of our world through these stories. We take on our own and create them for others.

How many times do we look at someone else and judge them by their actions while we judge ourselves by our intentions? We judge others by what we see, hear, and assume and we judge ourselves by what we intend. These scales aren't equal, and we do the same with our money stories. We judge and criticize based on what we see from the outside: how much others spend, what they have, whether they give back or not, what they're like as a person, and so on. We create these stories and form thoughts and feelings around those who have money, those who don't, and money itself.

When we're the ones who lack financial means, we might create the story that we're superior to those with money and if *we* had money, we'd certainly do something different with it. Let's be honest here: that's just a story we've created!

In the book, *Secrets of Six-Figure Women*, Barbara Stanny gives nine traits that underearners have in common. One of these traits is called "reverse snobbery" and what Stanny found is that underearners tend to have a particularly negative attitude about people who have money. Underearners might not even be aware of this reverse snobbery. What Stanny found is that reverse snobbery presents itself in a number of ways. Underearners say things like:

- I'd become less caring.

- I wouldn't work from the heart.

- I'm drawn to people who get by with very little. They have greater joy and less encumbrances. They're so much happier.

- People with money are unhappy.

- I think you don't see any people of great wealth having a lot of fun. Why? Because it comes with too many strings. (pgs. 58 & 59)

Maybe you can relate to some of these thoughts or have your own that are similar. Either way, they will hold you back because why would you want to earn more money to become unhappy, tied down, and uncaring? It's important to get clear on how we feel about people with money and rewrite these stories if we intend to bring money to us.

One of the reasons I set out to become a millionaire was because of my experience at fundraising events. Like a lot of young professionals, I didn't have a lot of money starting out so my way of giving back to my community was to volunteer my time by organizing fundraising events for nonprofits. I was doing good with the currency I had to give: my time. But at every event as I watched donors write $1,000, $5,000, $10,000 and even $20,000 checks, I knew I could do more good if I had more to give. Don't get me wrong; your time is valuable and if that's all you have to give, by all means, give it! But if you want to do more and create an even larger impact, money is essential. At the very least, clearing up limiting, yucky beliefs around money is critical if you're going to bring a strong, powerful, abundant energy to the table!

Shake Your Money Maker, Ladies!

Women are change makers and caregivers. We create life itself and we feel for others on a deep, internal, physical level. When I hear a baby cry, look into an animal's eyes or hear a story about someone or something that needs help because they're in an unfortunate place, I physically feel my response. It's called empathy and it's the ability to take on someone else's pain or emotions.

As women, we're good at giving and although it can be serving, it can also be harming. Many of our money stories come from a good place in theory, a place of empathy and compassion, from wanting more for others and a desire to serve others. But somewhere these stories got twisted up and instead of being positive, they turned negative. They turned ugly and became more about those who have money instead of those who don't.

Breaking Free From Scarcity and into Abundance

There are any number of things that influence our beliefs and feelings about money. The primary areas that keep us stuck are: experiences with money growing up, stories others have told us about money, people in our lives who have had an abundance of or lacked money, having money, not having money, politics, businesses and corporations, leaders, church and faith, nonprofit or charity organizations, and so on. Some of our thoughts and beliefs might be clear and others we may not even be aware of.

Often we come from a place of lack and scarcity of money versus abundance. You having money doesn't mean you're taking it from someone else. There's plenty to go around. Jen Sincero addresses the lack versus abundance mindset in her book *You are a Badass* when she says, "Believe that you can have what you desire, that it really truly already exists, and then go out and get it. Once you understand that we live in an abundant Universe, you can also drop the limiting belief that you serve the world better by not taking too much for yourself or getting too big." (pg. 209). There's more than enough to go around and when you take care of yourself and believe you're worth more, you can serve more through your financial gifts but even more so through your high energy.

Choosing BOTH/AND rather than EITHER/OR

Because of these stories we've created or taken on, we see money as an either/or proposition. For example, we think someone can be either a good person or a rich person, a person can be either a parent or an entrepreneur or philanthropist, a person can be either a good Christian or be wealthy. Jen Sincero talks about the either/or mentality in her book, *You are a Badass at Making Money*. She says, "We live in a fear-based society that totally gets off on cautioning us, on reminding us how difficult life is, on warning us how hard it is to make money, on holding us back lest we bite off more than we can chew, on screaming 'Look out!' instead of 'Rock on!' As a result, we've bought into this idea that it's better to limit ourselves than to stretch, and we've developed this fun-free either/or take on what's available to us: You're either doing what you love or making money, you're either a good person or a rich person, you can either help the world or you can help yourself, you can either go on vacation or pay your car loan." (pg. 107-108).

The reality is, you can be a great mom, philanthropist, entrepreneur, AND a filthy rich, kickass change maker all at the same time! This isn't about choosing; it's not about either/or, it's about both/and. Our hearts are the strongest muscle we have and when it comes to making radical changes and doing good beyond our wildest expectations, our hearts will lead. You already feel for others; you know you want to make a difference and do good while you're here on this earth, and it's going to take resources. Why shouldn't you have money? Why shouldn't women, who want to see good in the world, be the ones holding the purse strings and making the financial decisions? Instead of judging those who have money and how they spend it, wouldn't it be a much better use of your time if you created good energy around the attraction of and generation of money?

Isn't "Rich Christian" an Oxymoron?

In fact, it is easier for a camel to go through the eye of a needle than for a rich person to enter the Kingdom of God!
—Mark 10:25 NLT

This is a big one that held me back for years. I was raised a good Christian girl and from the time I was little, I was taught the verse about the camel and the needle and getting to heaven. Like so many, I interpreted this verse incorrectly. I made the assumption that rich people can't get to heaven because last I checked, it's impossible for a camel to fit through the eye of a needle. If you only read this one verse and nothing else in the Bible, that would be a fair assumption. But when you dig deeper, you begin to see a different story.

Rich people are not evil. Having money will not prevent

anyone from a blessed afterlife or, for that matter, a blessed present life, unless it becomes an obsession. This goes beyond the Bible and is important for everyone to understand if they desire to make more money. Money is just money and in order to bring more of it into our lives, we need to untangle our feelings around it. Same goes for keeping money; we need to release our tight grip around it if we want it to flow to us and stay with us. If money becomes an obsession (or in the Biblical sense, your god) that's when things become an issue. Again, it's all about balance here.

The Bible has a lot to say about money. In fact, there are more than 2,000 verses in the Bible that mention money. There are entire books about money and interpreting verses of the Bible. I am not going to go into a deep dive here but there are a few key takeaways that I pray will help you if you're struggling with desiring wealth and your faith.

The first thing we know is that we're called to be content with little or much.

Not that I was ever in need, for I have learned how to be content with whatever I have. I know how to live on almost nothing or with everything. I have learned the secret of living in every situation, whether it is with a full stomach or empty, with plenty or little. For I can do everything through Christ, who gives me strength.
—Philippians 4:11-13 NLT

A common misinterpretation is that money is bad and the root of all evil. This is simply incorrect and probably created and perpetuated by people who didn't have money but desired it greatly. Money is not the root of all evil; the obsessional *love* of money is the root of all evil. Think about a time when you desired something so badly that it consumed your thoughts and became an obsession. Someone could have a love for money whether they have it or not. In fact, I think it's just as likely that someone who doesn't have money can desire it as much as someone who has excess. A love for money can change one's heart and cause people to do things that are deceitful, illegal, and immoral. The reason the Bible calls us to be content with it and without it is because we need to be incredibly careful that money, or anything else for that matter, does not become our master. We must constantly check our thoughts and feelings around money to make sure we're balancing our motivations and desires.

Don't Give Away the Farm

Often when I'm talking to a woman one on one about money and earning her worth, she will talk about making more to give more. She'll talk about where she's going to give her money when she's rolling in the dough.

Recently, I sat down with a friend and fellow entrepreneur named Kaitlyn to talk about business and where she's headed. She explained that she's struggling currently but has huge plans for herself, her business, and others for when she is generating greater success. She talked about how she wants to start a nonprofit after-school program for underprivileged kids. She won't take a salary and she'll use everything to give back to those in need. As I listened, she went on to say she also wants to generate wealth because her parents are retired and incredibly stressed about money. She wants to increase her income so she can ensure they will be taken care of into the future.

Kaitlyn is an incredible person and we need more givers like her in the world, but she's currently struggling to pay the bills and make ends meet for herself. She shared with me all the ways she's cutting corners just to get by. She's very cognizant of any money she spends and often avoids activities like going out to eat with friends because it's a great stress financially. Her stress around finances is at an all-time high and while she desires to make more, she's only imagining where she's going to give money, not how she's going to use it to create her best life. Now, what I'm about to say is going to be unpopular but necessary. You can give money away, and you should, but not before you take care of yourself. Just like the oxygen mask on an airplane, what good are you to the world if you're on life support and starved of critical life-giving resources?

It is OK to make money and keep it for yourself. I'm going to repeat that because I'm certain many of you read over that sentence, quickly skipping past it. *It is OK for you to make more money to keep for yourself and improve your life.* Money issues come in many forms and I call this one the noble money issue. We justify making more because we're going to do good and give more. Again, there's nothing wrong with contributing to the world and making a difference, IF your plan is also to up level your personal life.

The same money issues keeping Kaitlyn without financial resources are the ones showing up in her vision to make money and give it all away. Her perception of people with money is keeping her from making it and influencing her plans for when she has it. She doesn't have it because her feelings are keeping money from her. Even if she did have it, she would give it away quickly because of her beliefs around people who have money. It's like the game "Hot Potato," just as quickly as you catch the goods, you pass it off to someone else.

My friend holds a negative perception about wealthy people, so if she actually made money, she wouldn't want to keep it because she'd become one of these people she thinks negatively about! These money issues have a sneaky way of preventing the natural flow to us. Again, you cannot become that which you despise. Therefore, if you see rich people as bad, greedy, selfish, or corrupt, you'll never be wealthy. Because why in the world would you want what makes those people awful? Instead, we create noble plans to give it all away, thinking that if we don't keep it, we won't be bad, too. It's a cute plan but it has a major flaw: If you continue viewing rich people as bad, you'll simply never have the wealth to give away in the first place.

Understanding How Money Flows is Essential if You Want More of It.

Having money is like anything else: a tool. And if you see it that way, making it not just about you, but about a way that you can play a part in the dynamic by which money is used for the betterment of all things, then having money is not only a blessing, it's a responsibility!

—Marianne Williamson

Rolling in the Dough is Not Only Awesome, But Totally Your Responsibility

Have you ever considered that making money might be one of the most responsible things you can do? The fact that you're holding this book tells me you desire more for your life. On some level, you know you're capable, even if you have doubts. You're learning more so you can grow. You had the means to purchase this book and perhaps others like it, to prioritize time to read them, and the wherewithal to know they would benefit your life. You're way ahead of the curve and truly fortunate to be in this position. All of this tells me that if you're not earning what you're worth yet, it's time!

Money is currency, a means of exchange, and like it or not, it's the currency of living. Those who have more can do more and hold more power and control—when we understand this reality, we can make choices from it. Not having money and not getting paid what you're worth is not serving you or anyone else. We need amazing, well-balanced people who desire to be great and do great things to have more money so they can inspire others who also want more from life!

When we lack the financial means to meet our needs, we have to rely on others. We might receive governmental assistance, local assistance, support from family members, or any number of resources. Those resources were designed to help people get back on their feet, not sustain their livelihood. But at some point, we started relying on them to support us. Even the most basic jobs that pay minimum wage are not meant to support a family. We argue about how minimum wage isn't enough to support families and that it needs to be raised, but minimum wage is just that, a minimum! It was never designed to meet the needs of thriving families. It's a starting point, a foot in the door, a first job, a stepping stone. We're not designed to stay at a starting point; the goal is to move up from that position.

You may be reading this and feeling discomfort in your body about what I am saying and that is OK. These are bold statements and I'm not talking to the whole world, I am talking to you, the reader with the brains and resources to hold this book. You were meant for more. We all know what it's like to feel stuck and stressed. Money is one of the greatest stressors and anyone who's been without it knows what it can do to a family, a marriage, a relationship, and our overall well-being. Money is energy. When we have it, we have energy. When we don't, we won't.

Not getting paid your worth causes you to bring a lesser self to the world and that is the greatest disappointment. It is our responsibility to make and have money because it allows us to be our best selves. When we're living our best lives and living out who we were made to be, we're doing what we love, making what we're worth, and contributing to the world energetically and financially. Contributing to life from that position is serving to us and those around us. You are more than capable. You were designed to thrive in a balanced, abundant way, not merely survive. When we decide to level up our lives, it not only helps us but serves everyone around us.

Let the Money Flow in and Then Out Again

Give, and you will receive. Your gift will return to you in full – pressed down, shaken together to make room for more, running over, and poured into your lap. The amount you give will determine the amount you get back.
—Luke 6:38 NLT

Regardless of faith, it is very important to understand how the flow of money works. Money is energy and flows freely to those who open their arms and accept it and also allow it to flow back out. According to Jen Sincero in *You are a Badass*, "Doubt is resistance, faith is surrender. Worry is resistance, joy is surrender. Control is resistance, allowing is surrender. Ridicule is resistance, believing is surrender." (pg. 227)

We've all had a time when we or someone in our lives has clung too hard to something desirous. This could be success, wealth, advancement, a promotion, or any number of things. The outcome is clung to so strongly that every conversation turns negative because they're miserable without that thing they desire. They have their heart set on what they want but they can't see what they already have as reason for praise. This state blocks the flow of money. Greater wealth cannot be earned by white-knuckling your financial situation.

It seems counterintuitive, but the way to attract the flow of money your way is to let it flow through you without resistance. The best way to do this is to give more. Giving money away, regardless of how much you have, allows for money to flow to and through you. Giving makes you feel good because you're helping others and it tricks your brain into abundance. If you're giving money away, it must mean that you have plenty for yourself. This abundance mindset is what allows wealth to come into your life. However, let's keep in mind that giving money freely because we're taken care of and therefore giving from a high energy place is entirely different than playing hot potato. If you're giving money away because you're uncomfortable with having it yourself, the flow will cease. There's an entirely different feeling when you look at your bank account and give yourself an imaginary fist bump for being awesome while figuring out how you're going to bless others with your awesomeness.

The same is true if you have great wealth and you're afraid to lose it. I experienced that situation after reaching my million-dollar goal. It was the first time in my life that I had a considerable amount of wealth and it scared me. John and I were on a plane taking a trip when I found myself overwhelmed with fear that everything I had become and built could go away as easily as it came. My initial reaction was to stop the spending of money, stop going on trips, stop buying things, stop any unnecessary purchases and essentially lock down our accounts. I was afraid it could go away, and I didn't have a plan for how I would replace it. I worried about our house, our expenses, our children's education, and on and on. Thankfully I picked up a book called *Rhinoceros Success* by Scott Alexander that reinforced the importance of giving. Money was never my master while I was working towards my goal; it was fun and lit me up. But once I had earned it, I slipped into the trap; money had become my master and I was terrified to lose it. The antidote was to give more abundantly and freely. Balancing the flow of money in and out of our lives is essential if we want to live free from worry and fear.

Invest in Yourself, You're Worth It

Because money is energy and it likes to flow, it's important that we don't hold tightly to what we already have. Similar to the idea of giving so you can receive, investing in yourself is also an important concept to understand. One of the mistakes I see many entrepreneurs make, especially women, is clinging too tightly to the money they have. This comes from fear of spending too much, not understanding how money flows, and trying to be fiscally responsible. Most of us were raised with the belief that the more you save, the more you'll have. And while it is important to plan for your future and pay yourself first through investments, it's a balancing act between living today and planning for tomorrow.

Money is currency, a tool to help us grow and build our businesses. Investing in yourself, your growth, and your passion or purpose is critical if you want to see growth. This investment can take many forms, such as hiring a business coach, support people, technology, tools, courses, or attending conferences. Our natural instinct might be to save and not spend, but that ends up blocking the flow of money. Instead, we need to release it, invest in ourselves, our ideas, and our businesses if we want to see them grow and prosper. Money is a tool and in this case a tool to help us grow and prosper.

Thinking about money as a tool, rather than as the reward, is helpful in understanding this principle. The purpose of making money and earning our worth isn't to die with a boatload of money, it's to use it to live our most fulfilled lives, help others, and become the best version of ourselves. When money comes into your life, appreciate it, don't pass it off so quickly like the hot potato, but in the same sense don't cling so tightly that it becomes your master. See how this can get tricky? Go with the flow, don't resist it, accept money into your life, give thanks for its presence, and then just as easily let it flow back out again, allowing it to serve you and others in the process.

You Must Grow More to Earn More

We're coming to the end of this chapter and while I could talk about money all day, I hope you're starting to get the idea that making money has very little to do with the money itself. The reason I love talking about money and am so passionate about sharing what I've learned is because to bring more wealth into your life, you need to grow. The equation is very simple and anyone can follow it: If you want to make more, focus on *becoming* more. To become a person of value, you must first become a valuable person. Those who grow and give back will earn the highest reward. It's not about the money at all; it's about who you become in the process. Reaching my million-dollar goal was fulfilling because I can honestly say I was no longer the same person when I reached it. There was always a millionaire inside of me, but I had to work and grow to uncover her. You're the exact same; you have a millionaire inside of you. It's up to you to let her out.

Journaling Prompts: Putting Pen to Paper and Getting Real

1. In order to break up with our money baggage, we first must recognize what's taking up valuable space in our brains. How do you really feel about money at your core? We might tell people we don't have any money issues and we desire success but if we don't get super clear with the truth, it will continue to hold us back. Here's an exercise to help gain clarity. On a piece of paper write at the very top: "Money is" and "Rich people are." Below those two statements, draw a line down the center of the paper so that you create two columns. In the left column, write everything that comes to mind without judgment. These statements can sound like: Money is evil. Rich people are dishonest. Money is power. Money is corrupt. Rich people are greedy. Now, in the right-hand column rewrite the truth. Based on this chapter and what you know about money, write what's truthful. These statements should sound like: Money is energy. Rich people are a blessing. Money is opportunity. Rich people are serving. If you feel yourself in a flow, feel free to write without rule, expressing all your thoughts and feelings around money. This exercise is to help rewrite the internal script.

Taking the Lesson One Step Further with Recommended Reading

The Secrets of Six-Figure Women, by Barbara Stanny

You are a Badass at Making Money, by Jen Sincero

One Action Step to Build Momentum

You're going to like this task because it's the easiest one we've had up to this point. Ready for it? Give to the next cause, fundraiser or person who asks you for a donation. That's it. It doesn't matter how much, just give and give thanks for the money you have that will bless others!

CHAPTER 7

Swapping Selling for Serving

*"I have never worked a day in my life without selling.
If I believe in something, I sell it, and I sell it hard."*
—Estée Lauder

The Best Salesman I Ever Knew

I DIDN'T REALIZE IT at the time, but I had a fairly unique upbringing. Like all kids, I thought my upbringing was normal because it was all I knew. But as I've gotten older and talked to others about their childhoods, I've come to realize that mine was different in some ways. My dad was a salesman in the paper industry, well before electronic communications prevailed and paper was king. We lovingly referred to him as a "pulp peddler." His role was to sell paper pulp, the powdery white stuff that looks a lot more like an illegal substance than paper, to companies that would turn it into the sheets we naturally imagine. He was the middleman, the contact between U.S.-based converting companies and primarily Swedish companies that harvested and produced the pulp.

When I was young, my dad traveled a lot for work. Most weeks he was gone for at least a portion of that week, leaving my sister and me to my mother's care. And like a lot of my friends' families during that time, my mom worked full-time too, so life was busy. My sister and I spent early mornings and late nights in childcare at our church or the local YMCA. I recall taking the public city bus between caretakers by ourselves from a very young age. We were deeply loved and felt that love, but we also understood that this was how life worked—Mom had to work and Dad was often gone. It was normal for us and we became pretty independent as a result.

My Dad's business customers were regular visitors at our family night dinners. This is how I got to observe his sales process. Being in international sales, my Dad had customers from all over the world. Sometimes we went out for fancy dinners but most times we welcomed them into our home and served them a family dinner. My dad said this was the best way to introduce them to our culture and serve them. He believed you could form a stronger, more genuine relationship if you welcomed them into your home, with your family, and served them a meal around your dining room table.

When we hosted my dad's customers around our dining room table, it transformed it into an international experience, a Magical School Bus of sorts. My sister and I learned about different cultures, food preferences, holiday traditions, familial arrangements, and how people lived in different parts of the world. I experienced firsthand what real business relationships should look like, and what a true, balanced sales experience should feel like. We didn't talk shop around the table. The dining room table was for creating genuine connection, understanding each other's similarities and differences, and service.

My dad was a true salesman. If you would have asked him

what he did, he would have answered, "Sales." He brought us into his career and his relationships through these dinners. Growing up, his example was my definition of sales and I unequivocally wanted to be in sales myself based on my observations. I truly thought everyone would want to be a salesperson based on what I knew of sales.

But as I grew up, I started to learn that not everyone has this definition of sales. In fact, few do. Instead, sales is defined based on everyone's individual sales experiences, and unfortunately often based on poor sales experiences. Sales is an ugly word for many people. A slick, pushy, slimy, ruthless, irresponsible, corrupt word. People define sales from the standpoint of being sold *to*. Everyone likes to buy, but no one likes to be sold to. The perplexing thing is we're all in sales whether we like it or not. We sell every single day and our careers, our futures, and our livelihoods depend on sales. We sell ideas to colleagues, we sell ourselves to customers and employers, we sell suitable behavior to our kids. Sales is simply understanding someone's need, offering a solution, and communicating value. Sales occur all around us and when done correctly, we don't even think of it as sales.

Entrepreneurship and Sales: A Marriage

What do you think of when you hear the word sales? Does it make you cringe? Can you recall a positive or negative experience? In reality, sales and entrepreneurship go hand in hand. The business you're creating is a vehicle. The vehicle can be in various stages of development and can be any make or model you choose, from a Ford pickup to an Aston Martin. You're the driver of the vehicle and sales are the wheels. The wheels allow your vehicle to take motion, going faster or slower depending on where you are. As the driver, you choose the direction, the course, and the speed but the wheels are critical for forward momentum.

Just like wheels on a vehicle, sales will move your business forward. Entrepreneurship and sales are directly tied because without customers or sales, you don't have a business.˙ Think about it: businesses are created to solve needs and capitalize on opportunities. When you've correctly identified a need in the marketplace, sales should occur when communicated effectively because people are looking for a solution to their problems. If we go all the way back to Chapter 1 and revisit the definition of a business, we find that Merriam-Webster defines a business as "the activity of making, buying, or selling goods or providing services in exchange for money." Selling what you have to offer and the exchange of money are not only critically important but necessary for your business to survive.

If you don't have sales, you don't have a business; you have a hobby. Hobbies don't need to make money, businesses do. As the entrepreneur, your responsibility is to ensure there are sales and depending on your role and the state of your business, it is likely that you are also the salesperson. Therefore, how we feel about sales is the foundation behind how successful our businesses will become. Are you following me? Now that that's clear, let's take a moment to check in with our bodies and see how we feel when we say, "I am a salesperson." Did you own it, or did you say it under your breath hoping no one would hear you? If you're like most people, sales probably makes you feel uncomfortable, which is why we're talking about it.

Why Would an Eskimo Need Ice and When Did Sales Become So Ugly?

Most people do not consider themselves salespeople. Even though we're all in sales, most would narrowly define sales to transactional—the actual buying and selling of products and services—when in fact, sales is much broader than transactional. Let's remember that sales is simply offering a solution to meet someone's need. The need may be clear or it may be unclear, but it can be uncovered by looking at pain points. When someone has a need or is experiencing discomfort as a result of an unmet need, a solution is desirable. Where sales has picked up a bad reputation is in cases when a transaction has occurred but there is no need.

We've all heard the phrases tossed around to describe a "good salesperson:" she could sell ice to an Eskimo or he could sell a ketchup popsicle to a woman wearing white gloves. We use these phrases carelessly to demonstrate that the best salesperson can be so persuasive they could convince someone who has absolutely no need for their product or service to purchase from them. Where these phrases came from and why they're used to describe a skillful salesperson is beyond me. Frankly, when I hear these phrases it irritates me and I often correct the person using them, letting them know that's not a good salesperson at all, that's an irresponsible salesperson.

When thinking about sales, too many of us think of some slick, fast-talking, boisterous guy in a fancy suit. We think sales is reserved for extroverts and people who talk quickly, loudly, and persuasively. We imagine used car salesmen, insurance reps, door-to-door vacuum salespeople, or the woman selling something online who won't quit bugging you to have a party. Most of us don't think of a salesperson as someone eagerly serving and going out of their way to help others. The reason is because we've all had bad sales experiences and we use these experiences to define salespeople as a whole. On the contrary, when we have a great sales experience, we don't define it as sales. Think about it: when you have a great buying/purchasing experience, do you refer to that person as a salesperson? Probably not. We usually say something like, "She was so helpful," or "He really understood what we were looking for." Truthfully, many people we come into contact with throughout the day play a role in sales. The waitress who provided great service during our meal, the pharmacist who recommended a product to help with our prescription, or our colleague who shared a new product she's in love with that we must try. When we have favorable buying experiences, we don't think of them as sales and we don't take the time to consider how sales touches so many different professions.

We've made sales an ugly word by defining it based on our negative experiences. Even words we use such as "closer" have a negative connotation and imply that the salesperson must be smarter than the buyer in order to convince him or her to spend their money. I don't disagree that some sales professionals have earned the negative reputation held in the industry today. Like any profession, a few bad apples can spoil the whole bunch. Unfortunately, when it comes to sales, the bad apples define the industry and the good ones are called something else entirely. This isn't helping the reputation because we need the good ones to offset the bad, but we're putting them into a whole different category.

It's time we redefine sales and stop perpetuating negative stereotypes. We've created an image of salespeople that looks like everyone's best friend on the outside, a charismatic hero who can convince anyone to purchase products and services they don't need, but with a sinister dark side entirely driven by financial gain at the expense of others. Because every single one of us is in sales, wouldn't we rather have a more compassionate definition?

Defining What Sales is and What Sales is Not

I am personally invested in changing the perception of sales for two reasons. First of all, it's critical for business and entrepreneurial success, but secondly, it's one of the greatest professions for personal growth when done well.

Let's break down the three main attributes of a great, balanced salesperson. These characteristics define the very best salespeople, the ones we need more of in the world.

1. Problem Solver/Communicator:

The best sales people are problem solvers. They approach sales not from the perspective of "how can I get more people to purchase what I am selling," but rather, "who needs what I am offering and how can I help them?" A business exists to meet the needs of its customers. There are problems and opportunities that exist in the marketplace where a business was created to provide a solution. Sometimes the problem is obvious, like in the case of acne.

Acne is the most common skin condition in the United States. It affects up to 50 million Americans annually and even more worldwide. As a sufferer of acne, I can tell you it is extremely painful, unsightly, and can affect your confidence and how you show up in the world. In 1995 two unknown dermatologists created Proactiv, the first multi-step treatment designed to treat the entire acne cycle. The need was obvious; therefore, the solution was highly desirable. By 2015, Proactiv reported over $1 billion in sales and at the publication of this book, it is the top acne treatment worldwide.

Other businesses are developed to meet needs that aren't as obvious, as in the case with the automobile. Henry Ford is famously quoted for saying, "If I had asked people what they wanted, they would have said a faster horse." Even though the solution to people's problems wasn't obvious and needed innovative thinking, when the Model T was introduced on October 1, 1908, it solved people's problem of needing faster transportation.

In both cases, there was an unmet need where a solution was created and thus a business began to meet the needs of people. Even when there is a solution to a need, that solution requires communication and an explanation of how and why it works. As in the case with acne treatments, the acne is the problem and the medication is the solution, but communicating the features, benefits, and how the product works is essential. In the case of the automobile, the speed of travel was the problem and the automobile was the solution, but it needed to be communicated clearly for people to make a purchasing decision. People wanted faster horses because that's what they knew; once they understood why a vehicle was better than the fastest horse, they were able to get on board.

The best salespeople understand the needs they are solving. They understand people's struggles and how their product or service can provide a solution. However, even when the need is obvious, the solution doesn't sell itself. We're quick to default to "it sells itself" when a product or service catches fire and it seems everyone is jumping on board, but I have never seen a product or service sell itself. The truth is that someone was effective in communicating the features and benefits of the product or service and as more and more people began to purchase it, they started making recommendations to their friends and family. We prefer to believe that the best products and services sell themselves because we don't have to credit sales in the process.

The most effective sales person understands their customer's needs and offers a solution through communication. In order for a transaction to occur, the potential customer must understand how the product or service meets their needs and value the solution being offered. The sales person can accomplish this through intensive listening and clear communication.

2. Service Provider:

Service is any action on behalf of someone else. If you've never been in sales before this might sound confusing, but service is critical to be an effective sales person. In sales, service requires thinking about someone else's pain points and helping to meet their needs. Service is putting someone else before yourself and continually thinking about what's in it for them, not you. It's turning the tables around and forgetting about your needs and instead focusing on theirs. This is challenging in general but even more so in sales, where there are quotas to meet and sales numbers to exceed. You are measured by your outcomes, which means too often you're focused on what *you* need to succeed rather than the people you should be serving.

In the book *The Servant* by James Hunter, being a servant is described in the following way: "Being the servant is simply the business of identifying and meeting the legitimate needs of the people entrusted to your care. Meeting their needs, not their wants – being their servant, not their slave." (pg. xviii) It all comes back to the Golden Rule: Do unto others as you would have them do unto you. Simply put, treat others how you would like to be treated. Sales is no different. Would you want to be sold something more than what you needed or be pushed, bothered, and harassed? Absolutely not! And because most of us define sales from the perspective of being sold to, why wouldn't we make this experience reflective of how we'd like to be treated?

3. Relationship Driver:

Sales and selling require a relationship between people. People will make purchasing decisions when they have a relationship with someone they know, like, and trust. Relationships don't happen overnight or in one interaction, they grow over time and through communication. Through his interaction with his clients, this is what my Dad was modeling for me as I grew up. Relationships are built on trust, which can be developed through genuine listening, concern for someone else, and honesty. Trust is imperative when it comes to sales. For a customer to make a purchasing decision, to spend their money with someone to meet their needs, they have to trust that the person providing the solution has their best interest in mind. And for anyone to know what's best for the customer, they must understand the customer.

Developing a relationship and understanding the customer's pain points requires the first two characteristics of a sales person: solving problems and providing service. Very rarely will a customer make a purchasing decision in the first interaction. It is typically as the relationship is built over time that they begin to trust the person offering the solution. The best sales people are in constant service to others to the point that when you're thinking about other people's needs and immersing your thoughts into what's best for them, you can't help but build the relationship. When you peel back the layers and really get to know your customer and what's best for them, you begin to serve them in ways that don't simply benefit you, which is how you build the relationship and form trust. When a relationship is established and trust is created, sales naturally occur because you're coming from the perspective of the customer and the customer trusts your recommendations.

4. Leader:

*"Leadership is not about titles, positions or flowcharts.
It is about one life influencing another."*
                                        —John C. Maxwell

If you're like most, picturing a salesperson and a leader would require imagining two entirely different people. But this is how we limit the definition of sales to transactions. In reality, any good leader is also in sales. In an article from *The Washington Post*, Daniel Pink, author of *To Sell is Human: The Surprising Truth About Moving Others*, says, "Spend a day with any leader in any organization, and you'll quickly discover that the person you're shadowing, whatever his or her official title or formal position, is actually in sales. These leaders are often pitching customers and clients, of course. But they're also persuading employees, convincing suppliers, sweet-talking funders or cajoling a board. At the core of their exalted work is a less glamorous truth: Leaders sell." We don't often associate leader with salesperson, but many salespeople end up in sales and leadership positions because they're naturally good with people. Again, we're imagining good sales people here, not pushy, slimy ones.

You might imagine a good sales person as the life of the party, the attractor, or the extrovert. Until very recently, we thought extroverts did better in sales because of their outgoing, gregarious personalities. We've also drawn the same correlation between strong leaders and extroverts, but we're learning that's simply not the case. In the same *Washington Post* article, Pink found that the correlation between extroversion and sales performance was essentially zero (0.07, to be exact). Introverts performed only slightly behind extroverts in sales, but it was the ambiverts who took the cake!

What's an ambivert, you might ask? Ambiverts are people who are neither extremely introverted nor extremely extroverted; they're somewhere in the middle. The reason is pretty simple and logical: extroverts tend to talk too much and listen too little, and introverts tend to be softer spoken and struggle to initiate conversation or ask for the sale. Ambiverts are a good mix of both and exhibit characteristics associated with high performing sales professionals and leaders.

Now if we consider that sales is far more than transactional and that all leaders are in sales, we can see why ambiverts tend to perform well in both leadership positions and sales. Good leaders and salespeople balance talking and listening, initiating versus pushing, and show a willingness to have difficult conversations. The best news of all is that very few people are either extroverted or introverted. Most of us are ambiverts, meaning we fall somewhere in the middle. Therefore, we're all positioned well to sell and to lead.

What if we looked at sales differently? In order for a salesperson to be great, they must be successful in their role and lead. This means they've increased the sales of a business and many people have likely decided to purchase what they're offering. They have many followers. People follow someone because they trust them, they have a relationship and they feel cared for.

In *The 21 Irrefutable Laws of Leadership*, John Maxwell defines "leadership as influence, nothing more and nothing less." (pg. 17) People follow leaders because they want to learn from them, they want to be closer to them. Their influence is positive, it's contagious, and it adds value to people's lives. The very first step in becoming a great salesperson is to increase your leadership. The best sales people are great leaders and vice versa.

In the network marketing industry, there is a phrase used

to explain why some people find quick success while others flounder initially. The phrase is that "when you enter the industry, you are either rewarded or punished for the life you lived up until starting your business." Essentially, if you prioritized relationships and serving others before, those relationships will pay off in your new venture. On the other hand, if you did not work to build relationships and trust, very few will listen to you when you come knocking about the next best product you want to share.

For the person who prioritizes serving others and building relationships, their influence is likely great, which makes their leadership high. People trust them and because they've already served those people, they will likely support their ideas or products. For the person who hasn't served others and built influence, they have more work to do. This doesn't mean they won't be successful, it simply means they need to start today. We all have the ability to grow in our leadership capacity if we so choose, which will help us as sales professionals.

Bringing it All Together: A Balanced Sales Process

We've all heard different phrases tossed around when it comes to the process of sales: you can't say the wrong thing to the right person, or the right thing to the wrong person, it's a numbers game, or any number of phrases. These phrases came from somewhere and hold some truth but are not gospel. It's true that sales is a numbers game in that the more people you talk to, the higher likelihood for success. But you can also churn and burn through numbers without considering the relationships.

When it comes to the sales process, it's all about balance. Balancing the relationships with the numbers, listening versus talking or presenting, short-term success versus long-term success, and serving others while staying focused on your goals.

It's all a balancing act and the most successful sales professionals walk this line with laser-focused confidence. They know what is required to be successful while also understanding that building relationships will serve them better in the long run. So, let's break down the role of an effective, balanced sales process and go through each feature in order to help improve our sales.

The Balanced Sales Process

There are three key areas that we're going to discuss about the sales process:

1. **The Foundation** (You, Your Environment, and Your Products/Services),

2. **The People** (Relationships, Prospects, Connectors, and Customers), and

3. **The Communication** (Presenting, Following Up and Converting).

Each of these areas will be further broken it down into the core components. Sales is a simple concept—one person taking action as a result of another person's influence—but at the heart of sales are people, which is how sales becomes a bit more complicated. In discussing each core area, I want you to balance this idea of sales as a simple concept with the complexity of people. Every time you feel you are getting overwhelmed, come back to the simplicity of the sales process. We will continually balance simplicity with complexity. All right, let's dive in!

1. Foundation: You, Your Environment, and Your Products/Services

Before any sales can take place, monetarily or otherwise, you must first understand the foundation. The foundation includes: you—the salesperson, your environment, and your products or services. You must have an understanding of these three areas as they stand today as well as an understanding that they will be ever-changing and evolving. In sales, as in many things, learning and putting into practice what you learn is important for true growth. Because sales typically involves a performance piece, getting paid or making some portion of your income only when you perform, it's critical to start performing as quickly as possible. Building this foundation is essential but that doesn't mean it needs to take forever. As you're building the foundation, you should be putting into action what you're learning. An example of this might be realizing you're not as well connected as you thought, so you Google "networking groups in your area" and join one that same day. Yes, that's what I mean by we will be moving quickly.

You – The Salesperson:

When people start out in sales, the first thing they typically do is build their knowledge of what they have to offer: their product or service. But the foundation actually starts with the person, the self. Who are you right now? Are you a leader? Do you have influence? Have you served others and built relationships? Remember the qualities of a good salesperson?

These are some foundational questions to ask yourself to gain an understanding of how successful you may be initially. Remember that you will be rewarded or punished (I personally prefer "not rewarded") for the life you live up to this point. We all have a certain level of influence or leadership and depending on that level, you will either be more or less successful at the outset. However, just like we discussed in Chapter 6 about money, you have the ability to change your level of leadership if you choose to work on yourself and become a more valuable person.

The first step in evaluating yourself is taking an honest assessment of where you are today and where you intend to grow. This is not a lengthy process and I recommend relying on your gut reactions as you're assessing yourself, but you're also free to ask others for help. What does your network look like today? Is it extensive? Do you have influence? Are you involved in networking groups or serve on an event committee or board? If the answers are no, let's start there. Get involved. Today. Find an organization to join or serve and get involved. The goal here is to make new connections and begin building your network, leadership, and influence. We have to start somewhere; don't overthink it.

If you're already involved and have an extensive network, start taking inventory of your relationships. Write down a list of the people you know. Once you have a solid list, ask yourself if you're ready to talk to them about your new venture. Even some of the most connected, influential people who seem to know everything and everyone get stuck at this point. Why? Confidence. It's scary to put yourself out there and let people know what you're doing. They can and many will turn you down. Some may think you're crazy. That's OK and it's actually normal. Believing in yourself and your ability to make good decisions (i.e., your new business) is a foundational piece of getting started. If this is an area where you're stuck, I recommend two things: building confidence and personal development.

Confidence is not something we're born with and it will evolve throughout our lives. This goes back to Chapter 2 and the sliding scale we discussed. Confidence is a muscle we strengthen through intentional activity. How do you build confidence? By trying new things, teaching yourself new skills, and growing in your proficiency. When was the last time you tried anything new? We all tend to get stuck in our habits and routines and unless challenged, we do not step out of long-held patterns. It takes intentional action (as you see, I say that a lot) to step out and create new routines and habits. What have you always wanted to learn or been curious about? Maybe it's playing an instrument, a new sport or exercise, learning to paint or draw. Whatever it is, and as unrelated as it might be to whatever you're doing, do it now. This will do two things: start to build your confidence as you master something new and form a new routine. Both the confidence and new routine are transferrable into your new business.

Personal development is the other critical piece we need to add into your daily routine. Although this can be for anyone lacking confidence in their abilities, it's also for anyone in general and is always ongoing. The minute you become an entrepreneur or business owner, personal development and learning should become a piece of your daily activity. According to Wikipedia, "Personal development covers activities that improve awareness and identity, develop talents and potential, build human capital and facilitate employability, enhance the quality of life and contribute to the realization of dreams and aspirations." See why this is important? Personal development takes many forms, but in the spirit of not overthinking things, I recommend reading books like this one in your hand daily, audiobooks of the same nature, or podcasts. Instead of listening to the radio while you're driving around town, turn your car into "drive time university" by listening to audios that build your leadership and life instead of mindless music and radio DJs.

The Environment and Products or Services:

This piece is straightforward: Know what you're selling, know what environment you're selling in, and understand your products and services. This doesn't mean take several weeks to learn everything you can so you can answer every single question. It means simply have a foundational understanding. You want to know enough to initiate conversations and get started. The goal here is to earn income while learning about your products or services. The reason I prefer this approach is because the longer we get stuck in the learning trap, the longer we'll stay there and make excuses for why we're not ready to talk to people.

When I started my very first business, I remember sitting on the floor of our brand-new office, without any furniture yet. All the business cards of contacts I had gotten up until that point were sprawled out in front of me as I made sales calls to people on my cell phone. We weren't even sure what we were offering yet! We were making calls to see what people needed and, in part, building a business around their needs. Talk about putting ourselves out there! If you already have products or services, start talking to people. You will learn more from their questions than from any type of training. Don't let the fear of not having all the answers hold you back. If someone asks a question you can't answer, let them know you'll find the answer and get back to them. They won't think it's weird if you don't *act* like it's weird—that's where the confidence comes in.

Understanding your environment is just as straightforward and you will build it as you go. Who's your competition? Who offers a similar product, service, or even opportunity? What's available on the market today to meet people's needs? Will they be using a similar product or service already? Understanding the existing environment will help you be more knowledgeable as you start reaching out.

2. People: Relationships, Prospects, Connectors, and Customers

The most challenging aspect of sales is getting your mental game straight. As I've mentioned, the best salespeople understand their customers' needs and focus on building relationships and serving others. You should always approach people with the attitude of "what's in it for them," not "what's in it for me." This is especially challenging in sales when we often have sales numbers and quotas to meet and exceed. When we're doing our jobs right and thinking about others, we're never relying on one person to help us reach out goals and pull through at the end. Unfortunately, it's easy to fall into the trap of getting our hopes up and setting our expectations on one person. It's easy to think, "Suzie Q is so close and when she pulls the trigger, I'll meet my goals." In this situation, Suzie Q often does not come through, we end up missing our goal, and we're upset with her when it's our business and our responsibility! Do not fall victim to this trap. Your business is to talk to as many people as possible so you're never relying on one person to meet your goals.

Building relationships is at the core of any sales role. Relationships take time and attention to build so don't expect this process to happen overnight; you're sowing seeds that will come to fruition over time, each plant with its own germination process. This mindset will allow you to feel a lot more peace throughout the process. Focus on serving others' needs and how you can help *them* before thinking about how they can help *you*. This isn't to say you're not responsible for your results. Everyone has different timing and you will come across people looking for the very solution you offer! In those cases, it's important they understand what you're selling.

This is the balancing point where sales is both a relationship business and a numbers game. In order to plant seeds for the future and take care of our numbers today we need to be in constant communication with people at every point of the decision-making process. At any given point, you should have people who are ready to purchase today, people who can connect you with others ("connectors"), and seeds you're sowing for the future. When you keep the focus on serving others and solving their needs, you will always be taken care of.

3. The Communication (Presenting, Following Up and Converting)

When it comes to sales, more people start with the communication rather than the first two pieces of the process that we've already discussed: the foundation and people. Only after you've built an understanding of who you are, what you're offering, and who it serves should you begin thinking about the communication.

The communication process is simply how you're going to connect with your potential customers and people in your network. It's in this phase that people tend to get hung up on the tools. Tools support communication and include the phone, social media, texting, email, events, video conferencing, etc. There are many, many different ways to connect with people and they will be ever-changing and evolving. The tools used are different for everyone depending on communication styles and preferences. What's important is building genuine connections through authentic, honest communication. When someone trusts you, they will be open to what you have to offer. I have found that face-to-face conversation is still the most effective, followed by voice-to-voice, and the very last is written.

In any sales process there are different phases. These can vary depending on what type of sales you're in but typically include initial contact, needs assessment, presentation, follow-up, and conversion. Depending on the relationship and timing, these phases can take more or less time to move through, but we'll go through each part so you have a clear understanding of each.

a. **Initial contact:** This is simply reaching out to the people in your network who you think many have a need for the solution you offer or be connectors to others. This step is inviting them into a conversation. Many times, this first step is written. It can be a text message, a message on social media, or an email. This step is *not* the presentation of your products. This is not where you outline all the details about what you have to offer. This is an invitation to have a conversation.

b. **Needs Assessment:** This is the actual conversation you previously invited your prospect to have with you at the initial contact. This conversation is best to have in person if geography allows, or over the phone or video conference. This should not be done in a written context. Written communication makes emotion difficult to decipher and often leads to misunderstanding. You want to have an actual conversation and hear the words, questions, and pain points your prospect is experiencing. Focus on asking questions to see if what you have to offer serves your prospect. You should be listening more than talking during this discussion.

c. **Presentation:** This step may take place during the needs assessment if what you have to offer is a solution for your prospect. You'll know when the pain points they're describing open the door for you to present your solution. The presentation is similar to the needs assessment in that it should also be in person, over the phone, or through video conferencing. The presentation can take place at an event, one on one, or through someone else entirely. This is where the process can change quite a bit depending on the product or service you offer. This is the point when you share information about your products or services and your prospect learns and takes in information.

d. **Follow-Up:** Follow-up occurs at many different points throughout the sales process. You may need to follow up multiple times during the period of initial contact to set up a conversation, or follow up the needs assessment to schedule the presentation. Often, the follow-up is what sets good sales people apart from the rest. Good sales people understand that people need multiple touch points to make a decision. Prospects have busy lives and it's the sales person's responsibility to get the solutions in front of them, not the other way around. Follow through on what you said you would do and follow-up to guide your prospects through the decision-making process.

e. **Conversion:** Conversion is the very last step in the sales process. This is where your prospect has shared their pain points, you've presented your solution, followed up with them to answer questions, and shared information. This very last step is asking for the sale, asking for referrals, and possibly converting them from a prospect into a customer. You would think this step is the most exciting for people, but it tends to bring the most anxiety because it requires moving the conversation to decision. Rarely will a prospect convert themselves; it is the role of the sales person to ask the prospect if they're ready to make a decision.

We're All in Sales

As we close out this chapter, remember that we're all in sales. Every single one of us is a salesperson because we're all leaders. How we handle our sales role will have an impact on those around us and whether we succeed in achieving balance. If we act professionally, lead conversations, listen, serve others, and help to solve problems, we will help change the perception of sales. We will also be more successful in leading and growing our businesses if we embrace our role as balanced sales professionals.

Journaling Prompts: Putting Pen to Paper and Getting Real

1. What do you think of when you hear the word sales? Does it make you cringe? Journal about your thoughts and feelings around sales.

2. Can you recall a positive or negative sales experience? What about that experience made it memorable for you?

3. In the Balanced Sales Process we outline three key elements: The Foundation, The People and the Communication. Which area do you feel is most lacking in your sales process today and which one is currently your greatest strength?

Taking the Lesson One Step Further with Recommended Reading

The Servant, by James C. Hunter

To Sell is Human, by Daniel H. Pink

One Action Step to Build Momentum

We can learn so much by observing. I want you to observe sales people in action this week. Intentionally note what they do well and keep track of language they use and how they serve you. These sales people can be a typical sales person or people we don't often think of as sales people: a waitress, a fundraising professional, a teacher, a friend. Observe how they serve others, the language they use and what they do to guide you in the decision-making process.

CHAPTER 8

Following Your Purpose to Discover Your Greatness

"The meaning of life is to find your gift. The purpose of life is to give it away."

—Pablo Picasso

The Choice to Live an Extraordinary, Balanced Life

WE'VE ALL FELT it at some point, the stirring deep within us that says we're called for something greater. There's something uniquely great inside each and every one of us. It's a feeling that comes from deep within that tells us we're here, in this time, on purpose for a purpose. Life doesn't have to be easy or running smoothly to feel this; in fact, it's usually not. Some of the times I've felt the deepest stirring were in moments of struggle. The stirring, while it can be unsettling because it's telling me to lean in and not to settle, is also deeply peaceful. It tells me I have the unique tools, gifts, and abilities to face the challenges in front of me and prevail. It has always led me in the direction of my purpose, even when the path has felt less than purposeful.

My stirring has come at inopportune and unexpected times, but it has always come. It's come in all sorts of forms and in different ways. It took me by surprise when I blurted out that I wanted to own my own business before I had ever given a single thought to entrepreneurship. It was thinking I wanted to make a million dollars when I wasn't even taking home an income. It was thinking I wanted to write a book long before I was writing anything at all. I've had many of these moments when I've caught a glimpse of the "more," the greatness out there for me and within me.

That little stirring can be clear, only to be followed by complete doubt, fear, and insecurity. For instance, I imagine myself with a bestselling book, standing on stages, talking to thousands of people. It's like it's happening right in front of me. I feel a high from this vision; I'm excited about the prospect of making it a reality. But then, it's inevitable; every single time I come crashing down to earth. I take a look around at my current circumstances, where I am right now, the structure of my days, how I spend my time, running around picking up kids, and I can't help but wonder how that vision could be possible. I know it's silly, but I even think about the clothing I would need to wear and therefore own to speak on stages and they look nothing like the Athleta yoga pants and cozy sweaters I spend most of my days in today. It's easy to look at our visions or stirrings and second guess whether we received the right one or if something got switched around in the universe—surely this vision was meant for a woman far more fabulous than I!

It's because of this gargantuan leap that many people don't even take the first steps to begin the journey towards their purpose. Couple that with the fact that life is busy, making it easy for us to stuff down our feelings and our dreams. In the hustle and bustle, it's not only easy to lose connection with your inner voice, your soul, it's actually more convenient. Let's be real; it's not convenient to get a glimpse of the life you were designed to live and then stretch yourself, working through all sorts of doubts and fears to pursue that vision! We intentionally stuff down the feelings because we think our current obligations and circumstances won't allow for us to follow a purpose. We have bills to pay and people who depend on us, so we believe we don't have time to pursue some grand vision, but I'm going to be straight: that's a choice. The stirring can grow quiet in these busy seasons, but it doesn't go away; it lives within each of us.

Our souls are guiding us in the direction of our purpose, even when we're not taking action towards it. Again, we are all designed for greatness and there's greatness inside each of us. Life is not easy but it was meant to be lived and lived greatly. Your soul is guiding you in the direction of your greatness; it wants you to pursue your purposeful path because it's in alignment with your gifts and talents and leads to the greatest fulfillment for your life. Your unique gifts, talents, and interests help shine a light on your unique path. The problem is that your soul can't do the work; it can only steer you in the right direction. The work is on you and the work starts with a decision to act.

We aren't born with a manual or road map so discovering our purpose is up to each of us, a decision that is solely ours. Many people go through life without living their purpose because it isn't required to live on this earth. Many people end their time here without ever discovering the life that was meant for them. It's not for lack of desire; it's a lack of taking action. Finding your purpose is not easy; it requires two things: listening and taking action.

Listening to your soul requires patience and quietness. Too many of us are addicted to busy. When we're busy, we can't hear our inner voice and we prefer that because our inner voice will most likely be the greatest inconvenience of our lives! For many, listening to your soul or your inner voice is like navigating uncharted waters. What our soul craves and what our human flesh craves are usually two totally different things. Once you have a vague understanding of your direction, you must act. Finding and living your purpose is an active process and can only happen through a balance between listening and acting. If you only listen, what good is the vision? If you only act but don't continue to listen, you'll surely head in the wrong direction. I like to think having this balance is like driving a boat. If you've ever driven a boat, you know that you must be in gear, with the prop turning, in order to steer. If you're in neutral, the water will take you in the direction it's flowing. If we want to follow our purpose we need to be in gear, not moving with the current, and in constant communication with our inner voice.

Do We All Have a Purpose?

From the beginning of time, humans have searched for the meaning of life. What is this all for? Why are we here? Here's what I know and believe: We're not here by accident. We didn't fall out of some tree and accidentally find ourselves here. And, if we're not here by accident, then we must be here by purpose. I am here on purpose for a purpose and if I am, so are you. If one is purposeful, all are purposeful. No one is here by accident. My soul and my faith tell me we're all here on purpose and for a purpose.

We're here on purpose but what *is* your purpose? Purpose is hard to wrap your head around and for many years I searched for mine without slowing down to actually find it. Remember how I told you stillness and meditation didn't come easily for me? When I first set out to give meditation a try, I was completely frustrated by my racing thoughts. I'd be thinking about what to make for dinner, what so and so said about me to someone else; I had an itch on my nose, my toes were falling asleep, and countless other fleeting thoughts. I thought it was a total waste of time until I learned that the goal is not to stop thoughts but rather notice them. What I noticed was that my mind was a jumbled mess and I was giving the entire mess my attention. I wasn't discerning between one thought or another; I was paying attention to all of them!

It was through meditation that I learned to stop paying attention and become intentional about where I allow my focus. This is what led me on the path to listening to my inner self, the one that was trying to guide me but was getting caught up in all the noise. There is a yin and a yang to all of life. A time to act and a time to reflect. A time to slow down and a time to move forward. A time for birth and a time for death. When we clearly see this happening all around us, we can embrace this very natural balance and flow. In order to discover our purpose, we must balance action with stillness.

We all have unique gifts, talents, and interests that help guide our path and uncover our purpose, but it's not straightforward. It's easy to get caught up in what others need from us, not what is best for us. The best way of explaining purpose I've heard was this: Let's say I am tired and need a rest, so I take a seat on an upright speaker. In that moment the speaker is my chair, so I might assume a speaker is a chair but that's not its intended purpose. When a speaker is used for its intended purpose, it projects sound. It can also be used as a chair for someone who is tired, but it is not a chair.

Living our purpose, which is the way to living big and balanced, is much the same way. We all have gifts and we are placed here on earth in this time and place for a purpose. Other people might see something different in us depending on what they need or want, but it's up to us to find our true purpose. So how do you find your purpose and are you currently off course? The first thing I want to assure you of before we dive in is that wherever you're at, it's purposeful. Everything that's happening to us is also happening for us, so the events of your life that don't feel purposeful yet might be necessary to finding your purpose, even if it feels like a detour. If it is your desire to live out your purpose and you're playing an active role in that process (listening and acting) then everything that's happening to you and around you is guiding you. I know it can be hard to believe but I will share a story with you in the following pages that illustrates how this has played out in my life.

Sometimes You Have to Just Follow Your Nose

I'm not one of those authors who knew she'd be an author from an early age. I didn't always have a pen in hand and an idea for a story working its way to the surface, turning over and over in my mind like a stone being polished by grains of sand in a rock tumbler. Nope, that surely wasn't me. Wasn't me when I was little and wasn't me through middle school, high school, college, or early adulthood. In fact, I avoided writing because I didn't think I was any good at it. I don't know why I thought this; I'd never received bad grades for my writing and no one had flat out said I was a terrible writer. I just didn't think I was good at it and a book sounded like the most painful, long, arduous process anyone could put themselves through. Why would you ever do that?

But I love books.

I love books like many people love cheese or chocolate or some other guilty pleasure. I love to read books. But I only ever read actual books, not eBooks or anything on an electronic device because one of the things I love most about books is smelling them! I do. I am absolutely, positively, completely and totally obsessed with smelling books!

I know people talk about fresh popcorn smells and fresh baked bread smells, but those are nothing compared to what happens in my nose when it meets a new book. For as long as I can remember, cracking open a new book meant first taking a great big smell of the pages. I love the feel of a brand-new book in my hands; I open it up somewhere towards the middle and joyously stick my nose right into the crease and take a glorious, wonderful, heaven sent, big ol' sniff and then I melt. I am convinced there is no better scent on earth than the scent of a book. Old paperback books have their special, slightly dusty or musty scent. New books smell untouched, the fresh ink on the soft, recycled-type pages. The Bible is in a whole class of its own and it's delicious and wonderful in only the way the Great Book can be. No other book smells like the Bible; they must reserve those slippery, thin, crisp pages for the book of all books. And the best, most wonderful book scent of them all is the textbook!

I didn't realize this book-smelling passion of mine was weird until college. I honestly assumed everyone loved the smell of books! For most, studying is a drag, a necessary evil of getting through college. But not me. Studying meant sitting down, reading and smelling and reading and smelling my textbooks over and over. I would read a few lines and then smell the book, read a few more lines and then smell the book again. I can't imagine what it looked like, but this odd behavior is now completely recognizable by my closest friends. Everyone who's ever seen me read a book knows I obsessively smell books. At first it catches people off guard and they look at me strangely, a question written all over their face as they ask, "Did you just smell your book?" To which I always reply, "Of course" as if compulsively smelling books is completely normal.

This book-smelling habit may have been the first glimpse of a portion of my purpose, though that never occurred to me. I just loved books and as I got older and started my path in entrepreneurship, my love for books grew to a whole new level. I realized I could either learn by doing over and over or I could learn from others by reading about entrepreneurs and their journeys. It started with *The E-Myth* by Michael Gerber, the first book I read about business. It grew into *Think and Grow Rich* by Napoleon Hill, *Good to Great* by Jim Collins, and *The Knack*, by Norm Brodsky. Eventually I started to amass quite the library of business and personal growth books. I learned how to be an entrepreneur by learning from other entrepreneurs in books.

Books have changed my life. They've opened up worlds for me that I would have never imagined, ideas I'd never be privy to and behind-the-scenes views of the worlds behind the most successful entrepreneurs in and before my time. Every book I've read has unlocked a door that was blocking something in my life. Every book has given me gifts I've carried with me on my journey like little tools in a toolbelt. I found my purpose through following what I love, even if it meant doing something that really scared me.

The Red Notebook

This book in your hands began to take root the day Sarah and I walked out of our jobs for the last time to start our business— my first entrepreneurial venture. We had just met with our former boss and were walking out of the building and leaving our jobs for the last time. It was exhilarating and terrifying, but we both knew deep in our cores that we were making the right decision. After we left the building, Sarah stopped before we got to our vehicles and reached into her bag. She pulled out a red notebook, handed it to me, and said, "This is going to be an adventure; start writing your book."

As she handed me the notebook, I stopped walking and just stood there, turning it over in my hands, feeling the flexible cover and touching the soft, gridded pages. I felt like I wanted to cry; I had never mentioned wanting to write a book because I didn't recall wanting to write a book! But when she handed it to me it felt like the most heartfelt gift, like she knew something I didn't. Something about this gift felt close to my heart; there's no other way to explain it. To this day, I don't know why she gave me the notebook or where the book idea came from, but I know it was purposeful. Had it not been purposeful, I wouldn't have thought anything of the moment and it wouldn't have touched me so deeply. The notebook and when she chose to give it to me were both part of my purposeful path. She wasn't telling me to write a book about getting married or starting a family. She was telling me to write a book about business, about being a young entrepreneur.

The notebook is still with me today, the moment it was gifted to me seared in my mind. But it wasn't until years later that I would start the process of actually writing the book. The red notebook was a placeholder for the book I would eventually write. I don't believe my only purpose is to write this book, but it's part of my purpose. My overall purpose is to help others on an entrepreneurial path and because books are the way I like to learn, it makes the most sense to start with a book. My God-given gifts are in business and entrepreneurship. By following my gifts, I've learned all about entrepreneurship and business and how to pass on to others what I've learned. One way to live out your purpose is to find your gifts, use them, and then share them with others to help them on their journey.

The Path is Purposeful, Even When You've Taken a Detour

My path to writing this book was anything but straight. I don't remember the specific moment but after about a decade of running businesses and creating my own entrepreneurial path, I felt a stirring to write it. The idea of writing the book had lived inside of me since I was gifted the red notebook, but I hadn't actively been writing before starting this book. I had been using my gifts to start and grow businesses, learning as much as I could about entrepreneurship and teaching other brand-new entrepreneurs one on one.

At first it was exciting; I was thrilled with the vision of writing a book. In fact, once I was conscious about starting the journey, I found all sorts of people writing books! This was exciting but it also caused some uncomfortable feelings of comparison and competition. I chose to lean into my excitement because I could see others doing what I felt called to do. I didn't have to simply visualize this in my mind; I could follow other people's actual journeys. But the competition and comparison showed me some unfortunate side effects of following my purpose as well. When you start to discover that path you were meant to follow, don't be surprised when you see others on a similar path but much farther ahead. That's what was happening to me and before I knew this was normal, I found it a bit discouraging.

When I started out, I didn't know how to write a book, so I did what I thought it would take: I started writing. I purchased a designated notebook to keep track of my thoughts and I wrote for one hour every day. My goal was to put on paper the ideas and lessons I had learned about entrepreneurship and organize them into an outline.

Month after month went by and my notebook was filling up. Some days I felt inspired and on fire; I would write pages and pages without ceasing. Other days I would question everything with fear, doubt, and insecurity getting the best of me. It was during this time that I learned about the role fear plays in finding our purpose. Coaches had told me and intuitively I knew that the closer I'd get to my purpose, the louder and stronger the voices of fear would grow, but this was the first time I was staring massive fear in the face. I hadn't felt it with my first company in the same way because we were in the middle of a recession. We didn't have many options and starting a business felt safer than employment at that time, so the role of fear was entirely different. Couple that with the fact that this book journey was meant for me and one I would be taking mostly on my own. We'll talk more about the role of fear in your journey and how to use it to your advantage later on.

I spent months and months writing and organizing but instead of getting closer to the book, I felt farther from it. The more I wrote, the more confused I became. Each new idea would lead to another idea, causing me to second guess the overall vision and once again reworking the outline. I was feeling more discouraged and insecure about my ability to write a book, instead of inspired and excited. In fact, when I went back through my notebook where I was keeping track of my thoughts, over half of the pages were filled with thoughts of fear about writing a book. So as the calendar year turned over, I decided to create a distraction that would pull me away from all of the confusion I was feeling with the book. I took a slight detour and decided it was the perfect time to build our dream home! (Insert eye-rolling emoji here followed by emoji sticking out tongue . . . my two favorites, smiley face, wink*.)

John and I had always imagined we would build our next home rather than buy. We wanted to build our dream rather than renovate someone else's. Within the first month of the year we purchased land and within six months we had hired a builder and drafted plans. The process was both time- and energy-consuming. During this time, I was still attempting to write the book, writing sporadically with no real plan. It was still in my heart but I wasn't prioritizing it like I needed to. I told myself that building our home was the priority and once the home was built, I would have the perfect environment to write the book. This, of course, was a lie and another excuse to put off my writing. There are no perfect times or perfect environments.

From the minute we put an offer on the land to the day we submitted our plans for approval, everything that could go wrong did. At every turn we faced difficulty, and not the normal, expected home-building difficulty. We ran into countless unforeseen, unpredictable, and even eerie roadblocks all the while I was dodging the calling to write the book. I wish I could say that I immediately understood what was happening, that I realized I was meant to follow my calling to write and that building a house was simply a distraction to avoid doing what I needed. But I didn't see that in the moment. All I knew was building this dream house wasn't going to happen at this point in time.

We changed course and instead decided to buy an existing new construction home. It was somewhat similar to what we wanted to build, and since we had our hearts set on moving, it felt like a safer bet than building. To be honest, we never fell in love with the new house. It wasn't love at first sight and looking back, I can see where we simply talked ourselves into it in order to move forward and put the building headaches behind us. But I was heartbroken about this being our new home. We moved in September 28, on John's birthday, and threw a party to celebrate, despite these feelings. We were trying to accept this new house as our home but instinctively knew it wasn't.

I went to bed that first night in tears. The breakout year I had set out to create was now a distant memory. The dream home we didn't build, the book I never wrote, the million-dollar goal I hadn't achieved, and my businesses were on life support. Of all the dreams and goals that I hadn't realized, the hardest to swallow was a check that I had pinned to the top of my goal board. It was written out to the humane society for $10,000, dated for my 35th birthday, on October 26. I had written the check in January and my intention was to turn it over to be cashed on my birthday. But along with all of the unrealized dreams from the year, that check would not be sent.

The Cost of Not Following Your Purpose

On October 28, two days after my donation was to be cashed, I received an invoice from our builder for all of the time they had spent helping us create plans for our dream home that was never built. The invoice was due upon receipt and totaled $10,000. The goal had been to give the single largest donation of my life and now I was faced with an invoice in the exact same amount. The same $10,000 I had intended for good was now being used to teach me a lesson.

Making the choice to follow your purpose is scary. It's inconvenient. It will likely disrupt your plans and will always make you do things that are uncomfortable. It will force you to grow if you lean into it, and through this experience I also learned it can turn your world upside down if you choose to ignore it. Since I didn't feel qualified to write a book, I wanted to instead create the ideal surroundings—a façade of someone who could write this book. Instead of doing the inner work, the hard stuff, I defaulted to what I knew, what made me comfortable. For many, building a house sounds scary, but not for me. Building a house, although a distraction from my true purpose, was exhilarating. Interior design and aesthetics are some of my gifts, so the decision-making process and vision are exciting rather than overwhelming. Writing a book was not in my wheelhouse; it was terrifying for me.

The $10,000 became a compass of sorts to get back on track. I knew something needed to change and I had a sinking suspicion I needed to face some fears I had buried. It was during this time that a woman who was just starting her coaching practice reached out to me. She knew a little bit about my story and wanted me to speak to a group of women she supported through coaching. I was flattered and we went out to dinner to discuss the event. Getting to know her over dinner, she was lovely and our conversation was effortless. She had a feminine energy that immediately drew me in. She was powerful but not in the loud, boastful way. She was softer, sincere, and peaceful. Towards the end of our dinner, I could feel a stirring inside of me that I wanted more from her, so I asked her, "Paige, you coach women one on one, right?"

"Yes, of course. I'm just getting started but I've built up a handful of one-on-one clients I work with and others in small groups," she replied.

I could tell she had no idea I was asking out of curiosity for myself. I was the established business owner she wanted to learn from, not the other way around, but something inside of me was saying lean in.

I asked her, "What does it take to work with you?"

Her face reflected the shock and confusion she must have felt inside. "Oh. I didn't expect this conversation," she said with the same genuine warmth and kindness she'd shared during our entire conversation. "I have two different levels, six months and 12 months."

"How much to work with you for six months?" I asked.

"$10,000," she replied. Her response was confident, yet it seemed new. I still wonder to this day if that was her actual pricing or if something inside of her told her that needed to be her price. I hadn't told her my $10,000 lesson. For all I know, $10,000 meant nothing to her other than a great client fee but to me, $10,000 symbolized a course correction. It was an opportunity to take back power over the past year and the detour I had taken. It was the easiest decision I'd ever had to make.

Without hesitation I said, "Let's do it!"

As I walked out of the restaurant, I felt strong. I felt empowered and I knew I had made the decision to take back control. I knew it wasn't going to be easy, so I was grateful to have someone in my corner who would support me. That one simple decision led to many other decisions that shifted everything for me. Through my coaching with Paige, we worked on purpose-driven decisions like getting my businesses back on track, but we also worked on personal decisions. Through deep conversations and soul searching, she helped me make the decision that we needed to sell our home and move again. We lived in our new home only nine months before we put it back on the market. It sold in a day and we moved in with my parents while looking for a new home.

Oddly enough, we ended up purchasing a home that had been on the market the entire year we were in limbo, but it had never sold and had been taken off the market. Even before we looked at it, I knew it was our dream home. The funny thing is we had saved this home during our search because it had everything we were looking for: John's garage, lots of land, a wood-burning fireplace, my tub in the master bathroom, an open foyer, two stories, and even a pool. The reason we never looked at it was because it was old and in need of many updates, and we thought we wanted new. The beautiful Kohler soaking tub I had imagined was now going to be mauve with brass fixtures. The open foyer had sponge-painted walls and cherry floors rather than the crisp white wainscoting I'd envisioned. Every aspect of the home needed love and attention.

With Paige's help, I also revisited the book I had put on hold. One day on my drive to meet with her, it occurred to me that I should ask her about tips for writing a book. We had been working together five months and our contract was almost up. I hadn't resumed writing the book yet, but it was ever-present in the back of my mind. We had a great meeting, talking for over two hours about business and life, and I completely forgot to ask about the book. As I packed up my things to leave, Paige stopped me and said, "I almost completely forgot! I have a friend in Chicago who's a writing coach. She reached out me recently because she's starting a writing workshop and I thought of you immediately! Because you're one of my clients and she's a friend of mine, I can get you in for half of the ticket price."

I just stood and shook my head as I said, "I came in today to ask you about any tips you had for me to start writing the book, but I forgot to mention it until this point."

"Well, I think you know what to do then," she said as she pulled up the enrollment site. "The price is $2,000 but you can get it for $1,000."

I didn't want to spend $1,000; I just wanted to write the book. But I also knew I couldn't brush this off. This was my path forward so without overthinking, I pulled out my credit card and enrolled in the course. That's how I met my writing coach and my editor. The one decision to hire Paige unlocked my ability to make all the decisions I needed to make to get my life back on track. Was it hard? It sure was! But every time I was following my intuition, following the path laid out in front of me and choosing to not overthink the steps, I was led in the right direction.

Finding Your Purpose is Beautiful But Pursuing Your Purpose is Messy

The fact that we are all born with gifts and purpose is beautiful. We were all made on purpose for a purpose. Isn't that incredible? Everyone's gifts are different and what each of us brings to the world compliments others around us. It's like a grand orchestra playing out in front of us and each of us holds an important instrument with specific notes and chords. The idea is idyllic. We want to be in that orchestra; we want to know what instrument we play so we can participate. But finding your instrument, pursuing your specific part, is anything but easy.

We glorify the idea of purpose. Because purpose is so beautiful to see lived out in someone, we wrongly assume the process of achieving our purpose is beautiful, too. But the actual path to finding one's purpose and living out that purpose is messy, risky, and ill-defined. It's laden with pain, discomfort, and doubt. Even though seeing someone live out her purpose is one of the most breathtaking sights, it's that way *because* it was hard and painful. And we see it in so few because the road is so challenging. Few actually take the leap to pursue their purpose.

Pursuing your purpose causes you to look deep inside of yourself to uncover your unique gifts and talents. It will cause you to march to the beat of your own drum and swim against the current. It's choosing the unknown over the safe and secure. It's going it alone instead of following the crowd. It will cause tremendous second-guessing, insecurity, loneliness, and doubt. We don't like to think about those parts of the pursuit when we talk about purpose. We'd much prefer to talk about the person who knows their purpose and is living out the path designed for them. We like the excitement of purpose, but we can't have purpose without fear and doubt. You can't find your gifts by doing what everyone else is doing.

Purpose is not a destination to reach, it's a journey. Purpose is walking a path that best utilizes your gifts and talents. You either polish or bury your gifts that were predetermined over time. The path doesn't already exist; you create it through your life. What matters is what we do with our gifts and the path we create with each step. The purpose of life is to find your gifts and use them. Use them to create you path and share your path with others. Simple, right? On paper, yes.

Living a Balanced Life Allows You to Uncover Your Gifts

We all have unique gifts, talents, and interests that light us up. Your purpose will most certainly utilize these things. When you lean into your gifts and follow your talents, you start to uncover how you might use them for your purpose. You'll know what your gifts are or can catch glimpses of them when you're utilizing them because you're enjoying yourself. Whenever we're utilizing our gifts, we find more joy in the things we're doing. Your gifts are things you did as a kid without even thinking about it. Typically, as we get older, if these gifts don't align with what we think of as typical career paths, we let them fall to the side. You might have thought, "When I have enough time, I'll pick that up again." Or, "When I'm more successful, I'll do that." But the truth is you should make time for your gifts now because they were given to you on purpose.

The biggest hindrance for utilizing one's gifts is rationalizing or overthinking. Many times, the alignment of our gifts and careers or how we support our families isn't perfectly laid out, therefore we don't prioritize the gifts. I once heard of a man whose gift was spinning a basketball on his finger. Talk about an odd gift! He couldn't see how his gift aligned with having a career, so he put it aside and went into sales. He hated sales and as a result never performed at the top of the organization. Eventually he decided to pick up his gift and bring it to YouTube. As the story goes, his videos got into the hands of the right people and he began performing at halftime shows. It started small. He performed at local high schools, which led to regional teams and eventually he had opportunities with the NBA.

Your gifts might not make logical sense, but they weren't given to you by accident. Too often we want the straight, safe plan. We want to go to work, make money, and take care of our priorities. That's not how gifts work; they can be inconvenient, unclear, and often not what we'd pick if we'd gotten to write the story. Bear in mind that you can succeed in doing things outside of your gifts, but you will never reach your full potential without employing your gifts. People will also use you in all sorts of ways to meet their needs, using you as a chair instead of the speaker you were intended to be. This will leave you unfulfilled and possibly resentful of your circumstances. It is up to you to lean into your gifts and build the life that was intended for you.

Following Signs and Clues

The crazy thing about purpose is that it can't help but find you. When we're not overthinking things, we can see all sorts of signs and clues leading us right where we need to go. Signs come in many different forms but the ones that have guided me in my life have included people, words or phrases, numbers, and reoccurring ideas. They've often come as those coincidental moments or the moments that stop you in your tracks. Those moments when you shake your head and think, that's really odd, I just heard that from someone else, or I was talking about that earlier. I don't believe in coincidences and this is why.

I believe everything in our life is working for our good and that we need to pay attention to the little things.

Numbers have been consistent guideposts in pursuing my purpose. There is energy in money and when a number, often financially related, hits me and something inside of me lights up, I pay attention. In addition to the million-dollar goal and the $10,000 course correction, I've had other numerical signs. What I like about numbers is that they're easy to grab. There's no mistaking one number for another. The number is the number is the number. They won't come as 50-ish or a million-ish, they will come as round numbers, keeping it simple in our minds and they will come often. Let's say $100,000 keeps finding its way in your path; there is something in that number for you. It may be an income goal, a savings goal, a donation goal, or any number of things, but that number is meant for you. When these numbers find you, pay attention. If they stick with you, they were meant for you.

People will also be incredibly helpful in guiding you on your path so long as they're not using you as a chair instead of the speaker you were meant to be. People will confirm an idea, plant the seed of an idea, or open doors leading to your purpose. You will know instinctively if the people in your life are guiding you towards your purpose or making you fit into theirs—the internal feeling you get will be your compass, so trust it. The red notebook from Sarah is an example of this. The irony is that the business we started together didn't utilize my gifts. I can do public relations, but I don't like it, therefore I was only going to be so good at it. But what I did learn through that experience was about entrepreneurship, my interest in business systems, and it started me on my path to my purpose. When you allow people into your life, accept their invitations, and lean in, you'll see that you can often use people to guide you into your purpose.

The last important signs that have become present in my life are those found in words, phrases, and ideas. Balance was one of these words; when it came into my life, it wouldn't release me. At the time that balance entered my life, I was living in a way that was anything but balanced, which was probably why it stuck with me. I knew it was meant for me when I began to hear it everywhere and it stirred something inside of me. It caused me to feel hopeful and when people would argue that balance was not possible, I would feel dejected and defensive. The same was true with business models and systems—when I started learning about these I was immediately intrigued. Most people don't know what I mean when I say business models or systems—they're the structure of a business and the way a business generates money. It was clear to me that certain models or systems could aid in a more balanced life while others would detract from it, and this intrigued me. Balance and systems go hand in hand because you cannot have balance without systems, in business and in all areas of life.

Surrender and Let it Happen

Out of all the tips for finding your purpose, this one might be the hardest for most people. We often think we're in control and in the driver's seat of our life. And it is true that while we need to initiate and follow through for things to happen, we also need to release and surrender. When I encounter someone forcing something, I can't help but think that it looks so hard and unenjoyable. There is another option: surrender. When you know you were made on purpose for a purpose, you can trust that all things are working in your favor to lead you where you need to go. There is a deep sense of peace and trust that comes with this release.

You'll know the difference between working hard on your

path and forcing it when things happen naturally for you. When you're simply working hard and there's stress and struggle and things aren't happening, you may need to reevaluate your path. Many times, people pick paths that weren't meant for them but make sense logically, maybe because of the financials or status. I love entrepreneurship and it's been a part of my journey that has led to so much freedom and balance, but it is not meant for everyone. I have experienced all sorts of people who want what they see others have and try to force it into their lives through entrepreneurship. They stress and toil and get nowhere. The journey isn't enjoyable for them or anyone else and the reality is that they're probably picking a path that wasn't meant for them.

Your path should be a joy. Don't make the mistake of believing life has to be hard to get what you want. Life is meant to be enjoyed today, tomorrow, and in the future. That doesn't mean you won't work hard or face fears, but when you're utilizing your gifts and you're confident in your path, even the hard work can be joyous. Don't buy into the deferred life plan model; we're never guaranteed a day and what a waste it would be to miss the life intended for you now.

The key to surrender is your mindset. First, believe that everything is working for your good and then trust that idea. When you trust this idea, everything that happens to you is also happening for you, both the good and the bad. And this trust means recognizing that so much is outside of our control. Understanding that today and every day is a gift. The fact that we're right here, right now is a damn gift and that's a perspective gift I was given when I lost Erik. You have nothing to do with the reality of being able to be here right now. In that same way, there is so much going on in and around you to support and guide you. But you will not enjoy all the supernatural forces at play if you don't trust and you choose to force it.

Trusting takes practice and doesn't happen overnight. You'll gain more and more trust as you see different events play out in your life, but this process takes time. The best way to begin leaning in is through stillness and meditation. When you slow down the mind to notice what's going on around you, you start to recognize the powers at play. It's easy to buzz right past the miracles happening in the busyness of life. They aren't going to hit you on the head and often times they won't stop you abruptly. Seeing and recognizing them takes a still, observant mind.

The Critical Role of Fear, Doubt, and Insecurity

The best recommendation I've ever heard for finding your purpose is to follow your fear. The greater the fear, the closer you are to finding your purpose. Fear is a compass in discovering your purpose. What you're most afraid of is often exactly what you need to overcome. Part of the reason you must overcome these fears is because they're usually the greatest resistance holding you back. Your fears may not make logical sense as to how they fit into your purpose, but sometimes simply looking the fear straight in the eyes and leaning in is exactly what it takes to overcome, move past, and discover your purpose.

There are two types of fear: rational and irrational. The vast majority of our fear is irrational, meaning it's not based in reality, but is completely fabricated in our minds. Rational fear is different; it's there to protect us. But very few of our fears are rational. Rational fears come into play if you're actually in danger, not "what if this could happen" type of danger but danger that is actually taking place. Women are great at creating irrational fears, we think we're doing everyone a favor and keeping those around us safe by worrying, but the reality is that we're stifling everyone and mostly ourselves! We hear a story on the news or a friend tells us something that happened to her neighbor's ex-husband's cousin's kid and before you know it, we can't stop replaying the scene over and over in our minds. Be honest: how many times have you changed a behavior or done something differently due to fear? Unfortunately, irrational fear makes up the majority of our thoughts, so even without being aware of it, we're letting fear-based thinking drive the majority of our decisions.

Our irrational fears are typically rooted in the fear of failure. What if it doesn't work? What if I look foolish? What will other people think, say? When I set out to write this book, I was initially very excited, but as time went on, I grew more and more fearful. I was afraid of all kinds of things and eventually chose a massive detour rather than leaning into the fear. The purpose of fear is to keep us safe but there is no reward in playing safe. They say success is a lousy teacher. We don't grow much when we're succeeding; we grow when we're faced with challenges and often through failures. Even understanding this, most of us avoid failure because it's painful.

Ironically, fear shows up and tells us it's there to protect us when it's doing the exact opposite. It says it's there to protect us from looking foolish, failing, growing too much or too fast, losing time, prioritizing the wrong things, the list goes on and on; but if we don't push past the fear, it wins. When fear holds us back, it isolates us, takes control over us, and quite literally traps us. When you let fear win and you stop leaning into it, it becomes harder and harder to push past fear when it creeps up, and it will keep creeping up after you let it win.

My greatest irrational fear that held back my life for years was a fear of flying. On one particular flight, just as our plane was leaving the ground headed towards Denver, I screamed and started crying as I grabbed onto my husband's arm for safety.

Out of love, he leaned over and calmly said, "You need to get control of this or I'm not flying with you anymore."

He was right. I was either going to avoid traveling altogether so that I didn't have to fly, or I would need to figure out how to overcome my fear. When we got home from our trip, I dove into everything I could get my hands on about overcoming the fear of flying and eventually found relief through meditation and anchor thoughts, as discussed by Mel Robbins in her book, *The 5 Second Rule.*

A fear of flying is irrational because the likelihood of a plane crash is very small. My fear wanted me to believe differently so that I'd stop flying and wouldn't potentially die. However, if I chose to stop flying, I would stop growing, exploring, seeing new places, and living my life! My fear said I might die but if I chose to listen to that fear, I would be choosing to stop living. Dying doesn't just happen when our life ends; dying happens when we stop living. Fear wants you to stop living and it's up to us to choose differently, to rewrite the script. Finding your purpose is much the same. Your fear will tell you to play it safe, swim with the current, go to school, get a good job, and be grateful for what you have, but you were made for greatness. You are here in this moment on purpose; this is no accident. You have gifts and a specific purpose to share with the world, so don't let fear win; do not play small.

"The graveyard is the richest place on earth, because it is here that you will find all the hopes and dreams that were never fulfilled, the books that were never written, the songs that were never sung, the inventions that were never shared, the cures that were never discovered, all because someone was too afraid to take that first step, keep with the problem, or determined to carry out their dream."

—Les Brown

Journaling Prompts: Putting Pen to Paper and Getting Real

1. When we think of purpose, we typically think of some grand, elusive vision for our life that takes a lifetime to discover. It's actually the opposite. Our purpose is so obvious that we often overlook it. What clues have been showing up your entire life that could be leading you to your purpose? What do you love to do? What makes your heart flutter? What does everyone say you're good at? What did you do as a child for fun? What did your parents think you'd be when you grew up? Write it all down without judgment. Seeds of your purpose are in there, trust me.

2. Are there numbers that keep showing up in your life? What is your ideal annual income? If you've never truly paid attention to numbers, start observing the numbers that come your way and write them down. They won't be vague; the same number will keep showing up. When you write them down, you'll start to see a pattern.

Taking the Lesson One Step Further with Recommended Reading

The Monk Who Sold His Ferrari, by Robin Sharma

One Action Step to Build Momentum

Take the next smallest step. Through journaling, you've discovered some things you love to do or you did as a child. It's likely you haven't prioritized them because they don't directly relate to your life now. We do that as we grow older; we start to only prioritize and make space for the things that impact our careers and families, letting all other joys fall aside. You're going to get back to what you loved. It probably won't make any sense. You might want to take dance lessons, learn how to play the piano or take art lessons and it won't make sense. Don't ask, just follow. Take the next smallest step to where you heart is leading you.

And, if you've stopped meditating pick that up again and recommit.

CHAPTER 9

Making Health a Top Priority for a Balanced Life

The foundation of success in life is good health: that is the substratum fortune; it is also the basis of happiness. A person cannot accumulate a fortune very well when he is sick.

—P. T. Barnum

The Top Priority That Took Me By Surprise

THE DAY OF John's college graduation, I watched as all the soon-to-be graduates ran around the auditorium to find their places. The auditorium buzzed with excitement and energy as everyone scurried around taking photos, imparting gifts, and celebrating the accomplishments of their loved ones. I scanned the caps and tassels, looking for John to have some idea where he'd be during the presentation. The band started up, signaling parents, siblings, and grandparents to take their seats. I had just graduated the year prior, so I knew firsthand the excitement the students felt as they anticipated walking across the stage after years of hard work.

I tried to recall the thoughts and feelings that had been running through my mind when I sat in a similar seat waiting to accept my diploma a year earlier. I had arrived late, thanks to the snowstorm that had hit the night before, so my mind was racing with thoughts of where to go, who to find, and the party we had planned for afterwards. A couple of my friends and I were throwing a graduation party immediately following the reception and I wasn't convinced we had ordered enough beer. If we run out, surely people won't stay, I thought. I wonder if we can quickly make a call to reserve more? My thoughts distracted me from being present in the moment and celebrating this incredible accomplishment.

It was likely that I was also thinking about John and looking forward to moving closer to him and finally living together in the same city. We had spent the last four years apart, never attending the same college because we wanted to ensure we would have our own experiences. Initially, we hadn't planned on dating through college, especially considering the distance. But somehow, we remained together from senior year of high school through the end of college.

I started college during John's senior year of high school. When I first left for school, we instituted a rule that we couldn't visit each other more than once a month. We created the rule so that no matter how much we missed each other, we would force ourselves to find comfort elsewhere, making new friends and experiencing true college life. We pretty much stuck to that rule though all our years in college. John joined a fraternity, I was on the swim team, and we both found our paths at our respective schools. The fact that we remained together was both surprising and expected at the same time. From the moment I met John in high school, I knew he was my person and our college years didn't change that for either of us.

As the college dean took the stage and the ceremonies

commenced, a soft smile spread across my face and I felt a couple tears come to my eyes, but I carefully wiped them away before they slid down my cheeks. I felt so proud of John's accomplishments and ours as a couple. Today marked the first day we would both be out of school and starting our careers. I, of course, had already graduated so I was finding my way, but an extra income would be helpful. We would be living in our tiny apartment with noisy neighbors, relying mostly on my income.

I hadn't quite landed the dream job I imagined after college. I had expected to be working in some boutique advertising agency, creating beautiful ad campaigns while rubbing elbows with important community leaders. Instead, I was schlepping newspaper advertising for the community paper during a time when newspapers were on a steep decline and online advertising wasn't a viable option yet. It was less than glamorous but I did well on commissions and had high hopes for the future.

Like most college graduates, I couldn't wait to be done with school. I was sick of constantly studying for the next exam, writing the last papers, presentations, and finals. During late-night study sessions, I would imagine life after college. I hoped to have a job I enjoyed, working Monday through Friday, eight to five, and then enjoying my evenings and weekends. It sounded like a dream compared to college: attending classes, working part-time as a waitress, studying in every nook and cranny and all hours of the night, and swimming while trying to also have a social life. I had imagined that the pace of life would slow down and I'd have time to enjoy it rather than rush off to the next obligation.

The start of the commencement address snapped me out of my daydream. A woman took the stage, shaking everyone's hands as she found her place behind the podium. I didn't catch her name or who she was; I just prayed it would be quick so we could get on to the handing out of diplomas and off to graduation parties.

"Class of 2007, it is an honor to join you today as you celebrate this momentous occasion . . . ," she began.

Her speech started just like all the others, thanking parents and grandparents for supporting the students, the college for turning out new grads, and congratulating the soon-to-be graduates on their accomplishments. She talked about what it took to get to this point: hard work, dedication, and a vision for the future. Then she began to talk about the future. I assumed she'd paint a beautiful image of what lay ahead for these graduates—job opportunities, putting down roots, starting families, and finally making money, all the things you imagine when you're approaching graduation.

But as she talked about the future, she focused on one vitally important aspect for success. One element that, according to her, if not prioritized and practiced daily, would cause all other aspects to fail. She said that this one thing held the key to happiness, fulfillment, love, success, joy, and everything else we imagine and desire for our lives: our health.

Her twist on the expected commencement speech took me by surprise. At first, I wrinkled my brows, uncertain about where she planned to take this topic and how far. I thought, Surely she isn't going to talk about health the whole time. I couldn't imagine there was that much to say about health and thought, certainly it isn't that important. But her entire speech centered around prioritizing health. Surprisingly, I found myself leaning forward in my chair, intently listening to what she had to say. I had never thought of health in this way. Like most young people, I took my health for granted. I had always been healthy, swimming through high school and college, which helped ward off the "freshman 15" and kept me active. I just assumed I'd always be healthy; I hadn't given it much thought. But her speech captivated me. This was a radical idea and in that moment, I could feel a monumental shift in my core.

She wrapped up by saying, "Without your health, you have nothing. So, as you move forward into the world starting today, plan not only for the best career but also for the best health. Take care of your bodies because you only have one to enjoy this beautiful life."

And with that, the audience began to clap and stood on their feet as she exited the podium. I stood along with them, clapping, my thoughts consumed by her presentation. This was not a new idea. In fact, it was radically simple, but it took me by surprise. As simple as the concept was, I had never considered my health at that level. I had never looked at it as the linchpin to all my other success. As the graduates were called one by one onto the stage to accept their diplomas, I was lost in my own inner world. I played and replayed pieces of her speech while thinking about what it meant for my life. I was no longer thinking about graduation parties and getting out of that auditorium, I was thinking about how I was going to take care of myself. I didn't have a health plan in place, and I realized that was a mistake; health needed to be a top priority in my life.

John and I have had many conversations about that enthralling speech throughout the years. It has changed the way we live our lives and the role of health and taking care of our bodies. I didn't realize it at the time, but it showed me the importance of balance and continues to play that role in my life today. It changed my views on success and what success looks like. She was right; without health, there is nothing. It's so critically important but it's also one of the first things to fall off of our to-do lists when we're short on time or too busy. Health takes time. We can't outsource it or delegate it to others. Taking care of our bodies is critically important and we're the ones who need to do it—no one can do it for us.

All Aspects of Health: Physical, Mental, Emotional and Spiritual

Health is a broad subject that includes many different areas of our lives. Typically, we think of physical health first: our bodies. Are we moving daily? What are we feeding our bodies to stay healthy and how do we feel? In addition to physical, there's mental, emotional, and spiritual. Merriam-Webster defines health as "the condition of being sound in body, mind or spirit" as well as "a condition in which someone or something is thriving or doing well." Health encompasses the entire state of our being—our bodies, which includes everything from our head to toes as well as what's inside: organs, heart, mind, and soul. Sitting in the auditorium at John's graduation, I wasn't thinking of health in this all-encompassing way yet; I was simply thinking physical. But over the years, I've come to learn that all of it is important.

When you consider everything that goes into health, you can imagine why it is a linchpin to all other success. There are aspects of health where we have control and others where we don't. Ask anyone who's fought cancer what the value of health is, and they'll undoubtedly tell you that it's everything. Health is the connective tissue in living a balanced life, connecting, and sustaining all other key elements. But unfortunately, like many things in life, sometimes we don't prioritize what matters most until we're faced with losing it. What is the point in having success if we don't have the health to enjoy it? I would argue that if health is not part of the definition of balanced success, what's the point in having success?

Each of us comes from different backgrounds and health records. We're not created equal and what a beautiful thing that is. We're each dealt a different hand of cards, healthwise, some more challenging than others. But each of us can make choices that tremendously impact our health, regardless of the hand we're dealt. For the rest of this chapter, we're going to focus on what we *can* control to improve our health, not what we can't. When we accept how we were created and the fact that we're all differently abled, we can begin taking care of ourselves. This is so important because each of us is uniquely created and none of us is the same, but when we accept who we are and how we were made, we can not only survive, but thrive. We've all heard of extraordinary individuals who are challenged physically but in spite of their physical limitations, they prevailed.

Take Nick Vujicic, for example, who was born with a very rare genetic disorder called tetra-amelia syndrome, which essentially means he was born without limbs. He is one of only seven known individuals in the world born with this condition. Despite Nick's physical limitations, he's created an extraordinary life for himself. He's an author and speaker who travels around the world, talking to groups and sold-out auditoriums about what it's like to create an amazing life despite physical limitations. Nick took control over what he could control: his mental, emotional, spiritual, and physical health. Instead of lamenting the hand of cards he was dealt, he is now a tremendous inspiration by leading a "life without limits" despite his differences. Each of us has the same opportunity every single day. Every moment we spend complaining about how things are versus how they could be is a waste.

At various points throughout my life, different aspects of health were more or less important to me. During my college years, physical health was critical in order to perform at my peak as a college athlete. I've found that as I've grown older, started a family, and run businesses, other areas of my health have also grown in importance. Mental health became a top priority while I struggled with postpartum depression after the birth of my first daughter and stepped through it with the second. Emotional and spiritual health have also become vitally important as I continue to build businesses and lead others. Physical health remains a top priority for me, moving my body daily through exercise and fueling me and my family with whole, healthy foods. Everything humans consume either builds life or contributes to disease, which is how I consider food choices in our family. When we eat whole foods, we're fueling our bodies with rich, disease-fighting super foods. When we're choosing the processed, convenient meals, we're often choosing things that lead to decay and death. Every decision matters, and every day we have the opportunity to make choices on feeding life or death.

Self-Love and Loving Self

We must pause here and talk about the critical importance of loving oneself. Until recently, I did not live most of my life loving myself or my body. In fact, I lived most of my life wanting to change myself and my body. For too long, my physical goals revolved around fat loss, body fat percentage, and muscle gain. Those are great metrics if you're doing it for the right reasons, but I wanted to change the numbers as a way of accepting myself, to be comfortable in my own skin. It wasn't until my mid-thirties that it occurred to me that I needed to love myself regardless of what the scale said or how I looked.

People set weight-loss goals for all sorts of reasons. Sometimes a weight-loss goal is important for health reasons but sometimes it's for appearance or comes from a place of lacking self-worth. We can get twisted into thinking that if we achieve those goals, we'll be happier, we'll love and accept ourselves. But self-love needs to be a top priority regardless of body size and appearance. Self-love is a gift we give ourselves no matter where we are, simply because we love ourselves.

This was a totally foreign concept to me when I started on my self-love journey. I had always loved myself within conditions: if I was this size, looked this way, achieved that goal, and so on. When I finally realized I needed to love myself no matter what, it was a long, painful road to correcting the mindset I had adopted over decades of my life. I finally understood that true healing and transformation had to come from a place of self-love, not self-hate. In order to fuel my body in the right ways and move my body for the purpose of strengthening my heart and taking care of myself, it had to be from the foundation of love. I could no longer use improvement or change as a motivator because when that was my motivation, I was never enough. By telling myself the numbers needed to change, I was effectively telling myself I wasn't worthy the way I was.

When we love ourselves just as we are, true transformation can begin. When we love ourselves, we begin to take care of ourselves in a whole new way. We move daily because our bodies are temples and we understand that it's the only place we get to live so taking care of it becomes a top priority. When we love ourselves, we choose the right fuel because we want to feel our best and ward off disease. I didn't understand this for most of my life, but I do now. It's been a huge, fundamental shift. I no longer use my body as a bargaining chip for love, or as the source of complaint. I carefully watch the words that come out of my mouth. Do you know how much time we waste on complaining about our bodies? It's significant! Try not talking negatively about your body or taking an oath to only say positive things and observe how many conversations take place around you regarding diet, weight, and working out.

The language I use now is, "I love myself, therefore…." I love myself, therefore I take care of all aspects of my health: physical, emotional, spiritual, and mental. As a mom of girls, I observe my daughters as they're growing up and want to live as an example for them of what it looks like to be a strong, confident woman in love with herself. That's uncomfortable, isn't it? But that's where love needs to start. If you don't love yourself, how can you show love to others? And if you don't love yourself, how can you expect to build the life of your dreams? You get what you give and the world is a mirror. Therefore, if you want love, you must show love and it starts from within. When you have love, you will see it all around you. So let's have love at the center as we dive into making health a top priority. This isn't about improvement simply to love and accept ourselves, this is about taking the best care of the temple we've been gifted, because that's how we can succeed in creating a rich, deeply fulfilling, and balanced life.

Creating Habits

> *"Depending on what they are, our habits will either make us or break us. We become what we repeatedly do."*
> —Sean Covey

In my line of work, it's not unusual to have conversations with others about how they want to change their lives. There's usually some aspect of their lives they're not satisfied with and they want to do things differently. In every single case, they are neglecting the areas of their lives causing them dissatisfaction on a daily basis. When it comes to our top priorities, we need to tend to them daily, with intentionality, balancing what's important now with what's important long-term. The eventual goal is to work on these areas until we've created habits. When we've created habits around our top priorities, we can truly see change happening without much effort.

So what is a habit and how do we use habits to create balance? A habit is a practice or tendency that we do regularly, almost automatically. These practices become so much a part of our regular routine that they would be harder to give up than to continue. We can all imagine bad habits and if you've ever tried to give up a bad habit, you know how challenging this can be. Now imagine your day was made up of good habits, habits to grow your business, improve your health, your relationships, and your spiritual well-being. When you've created habits around your top priorities, you will see positive change occurring consistently without much effort. It sounds too good to be true, but our lives are made up of our daily disciplines so when you're consistently implementing activities and practices that move the needle towards your top priorities, you'll see incremental growth.

In Brendon Burchard's book, *High Performance Habits*, he outlines what separates consistently high performers from the rest of us. High performance is defined as "succeeding beyond standard norms, consistently over the long term." Their studies found certain habits these high performers shared that set them apart. Creating habits isn't about making change happen instantly, although you can see change pretty quickly with improved habits. It's about changing your activities for the long haul to see changes now and into the future. These are activities you perform almost without thought; they have become habits to keep you on track and they shape your life.

Burchard found that not only are high performers thriving in their careers, they're also thriving in many areas of their lives through the use of healthy habits. He notes, "As it turns out, high performers' sustained success is due in large part to their healthy approach to living. It's not just about achievement in a profession or in just one area of interest. It's about creating a high-performance life, in which you experience an ongoing feeling of full engagement, joy, and confidence that comes from being your best self." (pg. 15)

Habit formation should play a role in all the critical areas of our lives, but health is one of the more identifiable areas for people. In fact, when we think of habits, we often think of health habits first: going to the gym, eating healthy meals, getting adequate sleep, drinking water, meditation, and so on. What I have found is that when you start to build good habits in one area of your life, it has a ripple effect into other areas. As they say, a rising tide raises all boats.

Foundations of Good Health

You cannot change your destiny overnight, but you can change your direction overnight.

—Jim Rohn

Health is a broad category, encompassing everything from your physical state to your mental, spiritual, and emotional well-being. It's everything we can see on the outside, the inside, and all the things we can't see that make up a whole person. Again, this is a big subject area so if you're looking to make changes, my recommendation is to start in one area, focus there, and then move to another. Your goal should be to create habits in each area so that the foundations of overall health are automatic in your life.

Health and its different aspects are a priority for top performers. Top performers understand what it takes to operate at their peak, and therefore taking care of themselves becomes a non-negotiable. And if we look at long-term success, health needs to become a daily discipline to avoid becoming rich in finances and poor in health, or as I like to say, a financially successful loser. It all goes back to Jeff Olson's Slight Edge philosophy and how small, incremental, daily disciplines lead to big changes down the road.

Physical: Physical health includes our exterior bodies and their interior parts, including organs, cells, muscles, tissues, and bones. Physical health is vitally important because we inhabit this earth through our physical being. If you think about it, you are truly nothing without your physical health. There are varying degrees of physical health and everyone is created with different abilities, but no matter what our condition, the goal is to take care of our bodies so that we feel good, have energy, and can bring our best selves into the world.

These aspects of health can be taken in any order and need to be prioritized depending on where each of us begins but are made up of these categories: movement (creating energy), nutrition (fuel), and hydration (water), together with sleep (restoration). Of course, there are many things you can choose from to improve your physical health, but these are the top categories I've found that help most people perform at their best.

Movement (creating energy): We should be moving our bodies in some capacity on a daily basis. Too many of us spend much of our days sedentary, so movement must be something we make time and space for in our days. Movement takes many different forms, such as running, biking, walking, yoga, stretching, boot camps, lifting weights, kickboxing; you get the idea. The important thing is to move your body, increase your heart rate, and get your blood flowing. Movement is incredibly important for all our internal and external structures. Keep things fresh by switching up your activities; don't do the same thing every day. Our bodies like change and you'll likely find more enjoyment if you're not doing the same things over and over again.

In addition to the physical benefits of movement, I love the community and mental benefits. Oftentimes, I will face a challenge in my workouts that pushes me mentally and physically. My brain tells my body I can't do it but when I decide to push through, I find that my body can actually handle the task. Of course, we need to know our limits, but more often than not we falsely limit ourselves. Whenever this happens for me, it reinforces my belief that I am capable beyond my mental limits for myself. Talk about a confidence booster! This is one of the main reasons I prioritize daily exercise—to prove to myself that I am capable beyond what I imagine, and that belief comes with me into my work. How we do anything is how we do everything.

Lastly, movement creates energy. I don't know about you, but I need all the energy I can get to make it through each day. When you're a mom, a wife, a boss, an employer, a colleague, a friend, a team member, a community leader, (insert your various roles here), it takes a lot of energy to perform at your best in all of those roles. Energy is not something we either have or don't have, it is created. We create energy to take on our daily tasks by moving our bodies. When you move your body, you feel better, plain and simple. Endorphins kick in and before you know it, your outlook on life improves by simply changing your physical state. Whenever I find myself stuck mentally, I move my body. Every single time I do this, I change my mental outlook or state. Your mind follows where your body goes.

Nutrition (fuel): We all know we need to eat well in order to feel good, ward off disease, and fuel our bodies effectively, but life inevitably happens. The biggest obstacle that stands between most people and their nutritional goals is time. For most people, time is the greatest challenge when it comes to nutrition because if you're going to eat right, planning ahead is an essential component. As life grows busier and busier, food companies have gotten smarter and smarter, offering our "on the go" families quick, easy and convenient meals. But very rarely is quick or convenient healthy. A convenient, quick meal here or there is not the problem; it's our reliance on these meals that becomes the issue. Again, it all comes back to balance.

Look, I get it. I am a mom; I run our household and my businesses. Life is busy and planning meals isn't always easy or convenient, but it's necessary and one of the most important things I can do for me and my family. Good fuel gives us energy and allows our bodies to function at their peak. We all know what it feels like to eat an indulgent, unhealthy meal. You feel bloated, stuffed, uncomfortable, and then tired. Your body isn't functioning optimally at that point; you're literally weighed down by your food choices. Now, imagine the opposite: what it feels like to eat a meal that fuels your body, gives you energy, and makes you feel good. Now, imagine that feeling becoming your normal state, the feeling you have all day every day because you choose foods that fuel life rather than decay.

Planning ahead is where most people struggle and where our health plans tend to go awry. This doesn't have to be a long, arduous process; it just has to be intentional. At the beginning of every week, I sit down and open my calendar. I determine how many meals we will enjoy as a family that week. I also take a look at my lunch obligations and determine how many meals I will be eating on the go. From there, I pull together how many dinners and lunches I will need to prepare for that week and put together my menu. To keep things simple in our household, I've saved meals we all enjoy as a family on Pinterest and flagged pages in hard copy cookbooks that sit in my kitchen. I grab the ones we want for the week and put together a grocery list, adding any other household items we also need.

It's not complicated but it does take planning ahead. Online grocery ordering and delivery has made this task even easier, and I take full advantage to save time and money. As a result of planning ahead, we also waste very little food because we're planning what we eat and eating what we plan. It's not a matter of "Do you have time?" It's "Can you afford not to?" Fuel has a direct impact on our health and well-being. If we're feeding ourselves and our families quickly and conveniently, we're not going to get much back. Nutrition is a long-term game and should be thought of as such. It's the secret to feeling good, having energy, thinking clearly, and bringing our best, most balanced selves into each of our days.

One final encouragement for all the parents out there. You will have the greatest influence in your children's lives over their nutritional choices now and throughout their lives. Often, we carry on the way we were raised and it's no different in nutrition. If your parents prepared meals at home, talked about the value of nutrition, and ate meals as a family, you will likely carry that into your home. If that didn't happen, you are less likely to do that unless you consciously decide you want something different than the way you were raised. Meals give families an opportunity to sit down together and connect. The food we serve our families during mealtime exposes our children to new flavors and builds a foundation of health.

Hydration (water) and Restoration (sleep): Two areas of physical health that you should never neglect are proper hydration and sleep. We all know we need to drink more water, but we hear different amounts thrown out all over the place. The rule of thumb I live by is half of your body weight in ounces of water each day. Water is vital for our bodies. It helps flush out toxins, hydrates our organs properly so they can function optimally, increases metabolism and helps us feel more energized. For most of us, it's the most convenient source of hydration available and it's free! The problem for some is that it's not flavored and people want something that tastes better. My personal opinion is to bite the bullet and do it for your health, plain and simple.

As our days get longer, our obligations get more plentiful and we often make the mistake of assuming we can pull extra time from sleep. We tell ourselves that if we get to bed later and wake up earlier, we'll have more time in our days to get more done. This is a very big mistake. In her book *The Sleep Revolution*, through careful research and data, Arianna Huffington shows that sleep is not only essential for our minds, but for our bodies as well. She states, "And science is now showing just how vital it is. Sleep involves a range of complex functions associated with memory, our ability to learn, brain development and cleaning, appetite, immune function, and aging. And that doesn't even begin to scratch the surface of what it does [for] our mood, our well-being, our creativity, and our relationships." (pg. 96) Sleep is critical and to operate at your highest level, it must be a priority.

Mental, Emotional and Spiritual: We are complex creatures and there's more to our health than just the physical. We also must be cognizant of our mental, emotional, and spiritual health. For most of my life, I didn't think much about these three areas. Of course, that's not because I didn't need to focus on them, it was because I thought I'd be fine without prioritizing them. I couldn't have been more wrong. Even though I was the typical emotional teen, stressed-out college student, and questioning twenty-something, I didn't know there were strategies to help in these different phases of my life.

It wasn't until becoming a mom and struggling through postpartum depression and anxiety that I started seeking help.

I was twenty-six years old and running a company when Wren entered the world; it was a recipe for breakdown and burnout. I vividly recall arriving to the office one day after dropping Wren off at daycare and having no recollection of how I had gotten there. In that moment I understood those stories of parents leaving children in backseats because I didn't remember dropping her off!

My mental health had been suffering. She was five months old and hadn't yet started sleeping through the night; she woke up every hour of the night. John and I did our best to take shifts but in our tiny 1,200 square-foot home, it was impossible to escape the crying. The result was two stressed out, sleep-deprived, anxiety-ridden, first-time parents. Sitting in the office that day, trying to recall the drive to work or the drop-off at daycare and failing to recollect either, I knew I needed help. I was trying to maintain this illusion of control—I was a young entrepreneur running a company and now a young mom. I wanted to be able to do it all. I already knew at that point that balance was important to me, that I wanted to run the business and have the family, but while the business was growing month after month, my family was suffering. My life was anything but balanced. As much as I didn't want to admit it to myself and others, I knew I needed to seek help before something potentially devastating happened.

I made a call to the one person I knew would listen, show love, and help guide me in what to do next: my mom. She cleared her schedule and met me for lunch that day. As we sat in the booth at a local chain restaurant, I told her everything that had been going on: the sleepless nights, the anxiety, the dread, the emotional struggles, and now the fog I was living in. I knew what I was dealing with wasn't quote-end quote normal. My instincts told me I needed to seek help. We both sat there crying while she patiently listened. I expected her to tell me it would be OK, that this was just a phase, but she didn't. She simply listened while nodding and letting the tears run from her eyes down her cheeks. I could see in her face that she recognized my despair.

"I need help, Mom," I eventually said.

And all she said was, "OK. It's OK."

I left our lunch and made a call to my doctor's office. I explained what was going on and they got me in right away. I recall sitting in the doctor's office explaining why I had made the call—that I was having a hard time—but also feeling the need to explain that I was fine. Admitting I wasn't OK and that things weren't fine was hard. I didn't understand that mental health is not black and white. My fear was that the doctors would think I was suicidal or that I would hurt my baby, but that's not what was going on. I just didn't feel like myself.

For example, one of the key identifiers that told me I needed help was my complete lack of interest in decorating for the holidays. That might seem like an odd example, but I went through Halloween, Thanksgiving, and Christmas without the care or desire to decorate our home or celebrate the seasons. I just felt exhausted by the task. Fall has always been my favorite time of year and decorating for the holidays is one of my greatest joys, but that year I just didn't have the energy. And I knew it wasn't simply an, "I'm too tired; I just had a baby" exhaustion. It was a deep down, depressed, hopeless "what's the point of it all" feeling.

When I explained this to my doctor that day, she got it. I saw a deep understanding and knowing in her face; this wasn't the first time she had heard this, and with compassion and empathy she told me she was going to prescribe medication. I wanted to fight it; I wanted to tell her I'd be fine and that I'd get over this in time, but I knew. I knew this wasn't something I should fight on my own. I was exhausted and no amount of sleep was going to fix my situation. I was starting to slip into a dangerous state of resigning myself to this new feeling. In my core, I could feel that this state was dark and it was eating me up. The goodness of life was gone, my excitement about the future was a distant memory and I didn't know how to get back to normal. I could not make myself care or feel anything at all.

So, I followed the doctor's orders and took the medication she prescribed. I was scared; I didn't know how it would make me feel and I was mostly concerned about losing myself, that the meds would make me feel like someone I'm not. But that's the life I was already living, not recognizing myself, my thoughts or feelings. I was hopeful that the meds would get me back on track and feeling like myself again. Weeks and then months went by. I couldn't feel a strong change but slowly, over time, my outlook gradually started to shift. It was so subtle, in fact, that I never even recognized it. It wasn't until looking back that I could see how the medication had helped me. It was the tiniest shift I needed to start seeing possibility again. The shift unfrazzled my nerves. I was able to hear Wren's cry without feeling like every fiber in my body was a live wire ready to go into shock. I felt more at peace and better able to manage day-to-day stress.

Seeking help saved me during this time in my life.

There's no way of knowing the depth of that statement. I don't know what could have happened if I had tried to "tough it out," but I don't want to know. I know what depression and anxiety feel like and I made the right decision in getting help. My story is not unique. Many people struggle with mental illness at some point in their lives. Recognizing the signs and seeking help is necessary but there are things you can do to be proactive in your mental and emotional well-being. Today, I prioritize meditation, devotion, and stillness to get in touch with myself.

When it comes to health, it's all about balance. When we think of health we often think about the food we put into our mouths. This is where balance is most apparent. Eating whole, life-giving food nourishes our bodies, but does that mean we can't indulge every now and then? Of course not, but it must be balanced. The same is true for physical activity. Taking care of our bodies requires a commitment today and every day that serves us in the long run. We can't make decisions that only sound good right now. We must make decisions that we know will support our health long into the future.

Journaling Prompts: Putting Pen to Paper and Getting Real

1. Where is your health at today? Honestly evaluate each area of your health: physical, mental, emotional and spiritual. Where can you grow? What new habits do you need to intentionally create to serve these areas of health in your life?

2. Write down five things you're thankful for today about your body and your health. We are all differently abled and your body is a beautiful gift. Do you celebrate the gift you've been given? Do you need to give thanks for your body and stop negative self-talk?

3. What excuses are holding you back from prioritizing all aspects of your health? Write your excuses down and then crumple up the paper and throw it away.

Taking the Lesson One Step Further with Recommended Reading

The Miracle Morning: The Not-So-Obvious Secret Guaranteed to Transform Your Life (Before 8AM), by Hal Elrod

One Action Step to Build Momentum

Start doing these two things today and every day:

1. Drink half your body weight in ounces of water each day.

2. Get 7 – 8 hours of sleep each night.

As far as greatest bang for your buck, these two actions will improve every single aspect of your health and they're the quickest to implement.

CHAPTER 10

The Final Game Changers

Twenty years from now, you will be more disappointed by the things that you didn't do than by the ones you did do. So throw off the bowlines. Sail away from the safe harbor. Catch the trade winds in your sails. Explore. Dream. Discover.

—Mark Twain

WELL, FRIEND, YOU made it to the end. I'm grateful you stuck with me and I'm thinking about you, wherever you are on your journey to becoming a balanced entrepreneur, whether you're at the very beginning or smack in the middle. If we were in person having coffee or a glass, likely glasses of wine at this point, we would have discussed the things from previous chapters, sharing our hearts with one another. We would have laughed and maybe even shed some tears over the twisty turns of our paths. We would have talked about what we love about being in business for ourselves as entrepreneurs, our dreams of the future, and most certainly our struggles with trying to do it all. How some days you can be on fire about what you're doing and where you're headed, only to be overtaken the next day with overwhelming thoughts of fear, self-doubt, and insecurity. It's normal and it happens to all of us. I'm with you, girl.

Have you ever been on a conference call or video conference where the training is recorded and then the recording is turned off at the end for questions? If so, you know that it's always when the recording is turned off that the real conversation happens. It's when people feel most comfortable sharing their hearts and the atmosphere feels less formal that the richness comes out. That's this chapter. The recording has stopped; now it's just you and me and our hearts.

These are the game changers that didn't have enough meat for entire chapters, but together make all the difference. This is you and me getting super real about what it's like to go after it all: the thriving, purpose-filled journey, the family, the exceptional relationships and a rich, healthy, beautiful, fulfilled life. This is us, sharing what it's like to be the balanced entrepreneur.

This is also the end of the book and the chapter where I want to remind you that it's not about the destination, it's all about the journey. As clichéd as it may sound and as tempted as you might be to roll your eyes, please just let that soak in. You're *in* it now, this is it, this is your life! As many times as you may have heard this sage advice, it's true. Just like we started the book, we're going to end it with this reminder: Your destination is not a guarantee. Nothing in this life is a guarantee. You only have right here and right now. How are you showing up? How are you showing up in your life for yourself and for others? Are your actions inspiring others? Is your attitude worth catching? I know it's tempting to focus only on where we're headed but when we do that, we miss all the richness in the middle. And do you know what that goodness is? It's your LIFE! Let's wrap this book up by refocusing on what really matters—the road you're on and the legacy you're leaving through your daily actions, attitude, gifts, and example.

I Do Hard Things, Not Hard Work.

When people ask, "How do you achieve success?" it's commonplace for people to respond, "Hard work," along with other words of wisdom. For as long as I can remember, this response of "hard work" has rubbed me the wrong way. It's always felt cheap, easy, and ego-driven. It's similar to the response of "good" when someone asks how you're doing. It's expected, it feels thoughtless, and it's just plain ol' garbage advice. It's also egotistical because the person saying it is giving themselves a pat on the back at the same time. This is because we value hard work, and even credit it as the backbone of the American culture. There certainly was and still today exists a place for hard work, but I don't think it plays as essential of a role in success as we perpetuate.

But what is hard work and how do you know if you're working hard versus simply working? One person's hard work looks very different from another's, and who's to say who's working harder? Questions like these caused me to doubt the old adage altogether and set me on a path to figuring out what the truth looked like in my life—similar to my journey around grasping for balance. The conclusion I've come to is that I choose not to see my work as hard. My goal is rather to work with passion and purpose, which involves doing hard things. When you're working with passion and purpose and your vision fuels your work, you see the work differently. You'll do hard things because they're purposeful, and when they're purposeful it shifts your reason for doing them. You will complete some tasks and assignments that stretch you outside of your comfort zone, but they don't have to be defined as "hard." I've seen it played out too many times—when the work is defined as hard, two things happen to people. First, they get burned out, and second, they grow resentful.

Burnout happens when you're working all hours tirelessly pursuing your goal. Do people work this way? Certainly, but I have no desire for that in my life and I don't recommend it for you, an entrepreneur who wants to have it all. Here's why. First and foremost, I don't believe people are effective when they're burned out or stressed out. Taking time to fill your bucket and take care of yourself is harder for most people than continuously working. Try this in your own life—instead of working around the clock, prioritize the things that truly matter: exercise, nutrition, sleep, personal growth, stillness or meditation, uninterrupted time with those you love, and so on. For most people, it's *more* difficult to make time for these things that aren't directly generating revenue. Our brains are hardwired for productivity so slowing down feels entirely unnatural.

However, I've experienced it over and over in my life and witnessed it in others—when we surrender, as opposed to forcing it, we often obtain better and more creative results. There have been countless studies on the importance of stillness, quiet, and even moments of boredom to cultivate creativity. Creativity is simply looking at a problem or task differently. Even if you don't feel like a creative type, you have the ability to come at a problem in a different way and think up different solutions. We strengthen our creativity the more we cultivate it, so the more you allow space to think, the more creative you will become in your thought process.

Whenever I'm forcing something, and I can feel when I'm doing it, I often think of a scene from my favorite movie, *Under the Tuscan Sun*. I can't help it; I'm a sucker for cheesy chick flicks and this is one of my all-time favorites. If you've seen the movie, you might recall this scene: Lindsay Duncan, who plays the role of an eccentric Italian woman, is talking about finding love. She's imparting wisdom to Diane Lane, a recently divorced writer who purchases a villa in Tuscany on a whim, hoping to change the direction of her life. She thinks of finding love like she used to search for ladybugs as a child. She would search and search for hours, not finding a single ladybug, only to fall asleep in the grass from exhaustion. When she awoke, she would find herself covered in ladybugs. The wisdom in her story is that sometimes when we're forcing it, we can work ourselves into exhaustion only to find that the solution or desired result happens when we surrender. I think of this example when I hit the wall from working hard.

The other thing that happens when we find ourselves working hard is that we can too easily become resentful. Think about the story above. How mad would you be if you were searching for ladybugs day and night without finding a single one, only to hear of a story of a girl who fell asleep in a meadow and awoke covered in them? We all desire to work smarter rather than harder, but when you're in the midst of working hard it can be incredibly difficult to see where you could be working smarter. By definition, hard work is exerting a great deal of endurance or effort. If that hard work isn't balanced with surrender and self-care, it's very easy to get burned out and resentful. When we're caught up in hard work or the pursuit of a goal, we tend to look around at other people's journeys and compare our paths to theirs. During such comparison, if we think it's coming faster or easier for them, we can grow resentful. You might be tempted to think this has nothing to do with hard work, that it's just about comparison. But when we define the work as "hard" we're often not taking care of ourselves at the level that's necessary and it's through that neglect that all the other ugliness creeps in.

You might be wondering at this point, if not through hard work, how do we achieve success? It's actually pretty simple. The first step is to mentally reframe hard work for ourselves.

Instead of calling it hard work or further perpetuating this piece of advice and its role in success, let's reframe it. Let's work with intentionality, purpose, and passion. Purpose- and passion-fueled work allows us to get into "the zone" or "flow," a space where time feels as if it stands still and you're so focused on what you're doing you forget you're even working. Many creatives will talk about getting into flow when they're deeply involved in a project and doing work that's purposeful. Flow gives energy rather than takes it away. How fulfilling would our days become if we were creating energy from our work rather than draining it?

In this redefining and mental reframing of hard work, more people will be called to participate in what lights them up. One of the things we don't consider when giving the hard work advice to future generations is how many might be turned off by this advice. How many hopefuls hear our hard work advice and wonder if they'll be able to have a family, go on vacations, and enjoy their lives if they desire success? Again, one person's definition of hard work is entirely different from another's and the belief that it takes hard work might actually stop more people from ever trying and discourage them from beginning. What if instead we said that success takes pursuing your purpose, finding the work that lights you up so much that when you do it, you're energized because you're making a difference in the world by sharing your gifts and talents? Who would rather do that than pursue hard work? My hand is up; how about yours?

"Unhappy journeys rarely lead to happy destinations"

A close friend shared a piece of wisdom that has stuck with me ever since. It was during a conversation where we were both sharing where we were in our respective journeys. I was sharing my struggles, where my path had taken me, and how I was feeling worn out and run down. Without any judgment, my friend simply said, "Unhappy journeys rarely lead to happy destinations." I don't know where he heard it from or whether he made it up, but it hit me and it so perfectly aligned with my balance philosophy. There are moments in life when a piece of wisdom or advice hits you and sticks with you and this conversation was one of these moments. What I realized is that the unhappiness I was feeling in my journey was causing me to be heading towards an unhappy destination.

Throughout my journey in finding balance through entrepreneurship, I have picked up all sorts of advice and quotes from people, articles, podcasts, interviews, and books I've read. The one quote that gets thrown around often for entrepreneurs is: "Entrepreneurship is living a few years of your life like most people won't so that you can spend the rest of your life like most people can't." It's a great quote with sound advice that has rung true in my experience to an extent, but too often it gets misinterpreted. The misinterpretation is that the road must be long, hard, and grueling in order for the years to be enjoyable, rich, and secure. That is not how I interpret this quote. Instead, I take it to mean that you will need to discipline yourself, create better habits, understand and grow yourself, make better choices in friendships, time, and food, spend time doing what really matters with the people who matter, and sacrifice some things today to have more tomorrow.

What it doesn't mean is that the journey must be grueling. In fact, if it's interpreted and lived out in that way, the destination won't feel any better. Just like the hard work versus doing hard things mental reframing, we have a choice as to how we live out our daily lives. Entrepreneurs are called to do hard things but what's your attitude in doing those hard things? Are your actions inspiring others? When you have a vision for where you're headed, and you live out each day knowing that what you're called to do isn't easy but it's purposeful, your energy shifts. Enjoying the journey is critically important if you're going to create an enjoyable destination. And enjoying the destination starts now because, as mentioned earlier, the destination isn't guaranteed.

Girl Power – Expressing Your Feminine Energy

Like many young women, when I started in my career, I tried to fit into the ways of the business world, ways which tend to fall more on the masculine side than feminine. The atmosphere lacked true feminine energy; people appeared to be more buttoned up, having it all together, and not showing much emotion. I tried to fit into this world; it was a slight shift from my authentic self, but I felt it. It seemed, however, that the more I tried to fit in, the worse I was at it.

In an effort to forge more meaningful connections and relationships with people, I would say things and then later recount them, wondering if I'd shared too much. On more than one occasion, I cried at work and then beat myself up for not being stronger. I constantly found myself trying to stifle who I was in order to be who I thought I needed to be to fit in. My language, my clothing, my mannerisms, and my behavior all shifted slightly to fit into this new world and not make waves.

When I look back, I feel sorry for this version of myself. When people ask, "What advice would you give your younger self?" I know my answer instantly. I would tell myself to *be* myself and be confident in who I am. I did not understand the ways of the business world and I didn't want to do anything that would make me look foolish, but in my desperate attempt to fit in, I lost myself. Whenever we try to fit in, we diminish the special and unique parts of ourselves that make us really great. I didn't stand out; I shrank in order to fit in.

Women and men were created differently. We have different strengths and when it comes to business, feminine strengths aren't as outwardly appreciated yet, because it's still primarily a "man's world." Depending on which industry you find yourself in, this may be more or less true. I find it in entrepreneurship— it's still very true but starting to shift. I celebrate that change and my hope is that we continue to see more women stepping into entrepreneurship. But I want to see them bring their unique strengths and feminine gifts right alongside them, unapologetically.

As women, we tend to feel more emotionally, and we're often caregivers because we see other's needs and want to help. We're relationship builders and we create more meaningful, deeper, more personal relationships with others. These relationships are stronger than their surface-level counterparts. We love and care and sometimes these deep feelings cause us to react more strongly than we'd like, but in the end, it lets people know how we feel and that's a good thing. These are great strengths in business. Instead of seeing crying over business as a negative, why don't we see it as a positive? It means we care, it means we feel, and it means it's important to us. When did this become a bad thing?

Business is personal for me. It's personal because it's tied to my purpose; it's doing the will of God in my life so of course I feel deeply about it. I have shifted from trying not to cry at work or in business to crying almost every single day and I'm not exaggerating. Hell! If I have a day where I don't cry or at the very least tear up, I know my heart wasn't in it. When my heart is involved, and that's my hope every single day, I react with emotion. We deem having an emotional response as a negative thing, but I've learned how to tap into this emotional energy in a way that it now drives my decisions and behaviors and has made all the difference in my business. Business is often tied to our unique gifts and talents so when we're using those gifts to their full extent, our soul will be on fire. When you're using your gifts, serving others, and making a massive difference, your response can't help but be emotional!

Here's the catch, however. Sometimes in an effort to be more feminine and bring more emotion and heart to business, things can get a little twisty. Early on in my efforts to be more feminine, feel more deeply, and express my emotions, I found myself twisted up in the negative side of feminine energy. Now ladies, can we jointly admit that some of our feminine ways aren't always positive or serving? What am I referring to? I'm talking about comparison, judgment, competition, and gossip. Let's be super straight: we tend to bring some of these not-so-nice things to the table that our male counterparts don't always share. I have compassion for women though, because I find that many of these negative behaviors are rooted in something that breaks my heart: a lack of self-confidence. When we're judging another sister or stuck in comparison, it's usually because we're lacking our own confidence.

You Gotta Love Yourself in Order to Show Love to Others.

"It's impossible to consistently behave in a manner inconsistent with how we see ourselves. We can do very few things in a positive way if we feel negative about ourselves."
—Zig Ziglar

We started talking about this in the previous chapter, but it's such a game changer that it deserves space in this chapter, too. Remember how I told you I started writing this book and then gave it up because I got trapped in all sorts of fear and self-doubt? Well it was because I had found my purpose and when you find your purpose, fear will come right alongside, sitting in the passenger seat, eager to yell "Watch out!" at every twist and turn. The way to put this fear in its place is to be confident in who you are, your gifts, your purpose here on earth, and show love for yourself without conditions. Well, I didn't have that love for myself when I started this book. My love for myself was conditional; if I made it to the gym every day, if I did a good job in my work, if I was making money, if I was exceeding other's expectations of me, if I was making good nutritional choices, if I wasn't gaining weight, so on and so forth.

It wasn't until the turn of the calendar year when I was noodling my goals for the new year and figuring out my health and fitness goals that it hit me hard. It hit me so hard I found myself on my back again, lying on the floor of my closet, looking at the ceiling, ugly crying. I realized what I desperately needed and wanted: to love myself completely, without conditions, without expectations, just love myself. I was thirty-five years old and it was the first time this thought had even occurred to me. I can say with sincere honesty and gut-wrenching, heartbreaking, true admission that it had never occurred to me that loving myself was a requirement for everything else.

That day, lying on the floor of my closet, I set a whole new goal for myself. I was going to figure out how to love myself. It wasn't easy, people. When you don't love yourself, you create all sorts of nasty habits. I would say things to myself that I would never, under any circumstances, say to anyone else. I criticized my appearance; I mentally recounted all the areas of my body that needed toning, trimming, and less squish. I pinched my sides, the back of my arms and my thighs, reminding myself of how much work I had to do. I mentally took note of how my clothes fit, how my body felt, how I wanted to look, feel, and on and on. This obsession over my physical appearance started in middle school and through the years had grown to dangerous proportions. I criticized my physical self, but the criticism was an extension of all the ways I felt inadequate.

When I made it my mission to change my internal dialogue, I had to first take it minute by minute, consciously changing my internal voice. At least every 10 minutes, maybe more often than that, I had to deliberately shift my language. I intentionally shifted my critical internal voice to "but I'm choosing to love myself anyway." Many times, the mental shift wasn't enough. The negative voice would continue, so I had to physically shift. My physical shift took the place of lying on my back on the floor looking at the ceiling. This allowed me to stop, shift my perspective, feel the support of the earth and change my thinking. John came to understand what I was doing, and he supported this shift and saw, by my physical position, how difficult this change was for me.

The other thing that helped make the shift was taking a long view, an end of life perspective. I reminded myself that at the end of my life, on my deathbed, I will not wish that I had spent more time obsessing about my body. I'd already wasted too much time and it was time to make a change. Often my brain wouldn't listen, and I would need to say out loud "no!" in order to stop the mental spin. I applied the same rule to myself that we all learn as children: if you don't have anything nice to say, don't say anything at all. This meant no self-deprecating talk about myself to girlfriends and nothing internal. I went months and months without looking at my body in the mirror because that was a source of negative thoughts. I didn't look at my body in a mirror until I had something nice to think about it; I could appreciate the temple I was given, and I could see it for all the glorious beauty it was. Lastly, I forced a new soundtrack, literally. I started listening to songs that celebrate the beautiful creatures we were made to be like "This is Me" by Keala Settle, "Me Too" by Meghan Trainor and "You Say" by Lauren Daigle, and I let the words sink in. Like really sink in, until I was singing along at the top of my lungs in my car, by myself. I borrowed the confidence in the songs until I felt the confidence in myself.

Ever so slowly, the dialogue I was rehearsing over and over started to take root. I started to feel the love I was showing myself and I started to believe it. I started to love myself without conditions, without expectations, just me. I still have moments when I fall into old bad habits and catch myself in a negative mental dialogue, but today I catch it quickly and shift it immediately. I love myself now. It was the necessary shift I needed to make in order to write this book, serve others, and build a rock-solid base of self-confidence. It's the same thing you need to do if you're going to pursue your purpose in a balanced, whole-life way.

According to John Maxwell in his book, *The 15 Invaluable Laws of Growth*, "Self-esteem is the single most significant key to a person's behavior." (pg. 39) Read that again, because it's eye-opening, the single most significant key. It's not just one of the keys, self-esteem is THE key. I didn't know this when I went on my self-love journey to change the way I talked to myself, but I can testify to the difference it has made in my life. Simply put, if you don't love yourself, why would you deem yourself worth of pursuing your purpose? If you don't love yourself, you can't see value in yourself, and what you have to offer the world. It's everything.

The world will reflect what we see and what we give. If we don't have love for ourselves, how will we receive love from others? Loving yourself first is the prerequisite to loving others and receiving love! And here's why this is important to pursuing your purpose—pursuing your purpose is scary; it's vulnerable, like showing the world your raw, real, naked self. It's saying to the world, "World! Here are my unique gifts and talents; here's what I have to offer, whatdoya think!?" That's scary as hell and you need love when you do it. You, friend, are going to need to love yourself because you *will* do it, that's why you're reading this book! To design your balanced, wonderful life! Do not go through this life without sharing with the world everything you were given and the glorious gifts you have; do not hide them from the world. The single most important key to sharing all the gifts you were gifted, right here, right now, and to change the world around you, is love. And that love has to start within. Yep, it's that important sister.

Stop Eating Poison

There's a funny thing happens when you begin to pursue your purpose: You'll start to find all sorts of people seemingly doing the same damn thing. And you know what will happen? This is what you'll tell yourself: "Ohmygosh, it's already being done. Everything I thought I was supposed to do is already happening and they're doing it WAY better than I ever could! Who am I kidding? What was I thinking!? I can't do what they're doing as good as they're doing it, so why would I even try? Welp, better start thinking about something else I can offer that's not already been taken." Yep, we're back to comparison.

I know this thought process because it's happened a thousand times in my head. Do you know how many incredible, untouchable people have written books, spoken on stages, and helped women in a similar capacity that I'm being called to do? A boatload! At first it scared me to death and created a jumbled mess of self-sabotaging, limiting beliefs in my head. I thought,

"Who the hell am I to compete with these incredible, kick-ass, highly accomplished, beautiful (because your brain will throw that in there) women!?" But I had it wrong. I wasn't supposed to be seeing them as competition. I was swallowing the poison pill of comparison.

Guess what happens when you compare yourself to someone else? You find all the ways they're kicking ass and all the ways you suck. You look at their accomplishments and your failures. Not only is it not a fair comparison, but you weren't supposed to compare in the first place! If we really boil it down, you're actually being a spoiled jerk and making the whole thing all about you. Look, I'm not trying to be mean here; I'm calling it out in you because I've done this time and again. I've made other people's accomplishments about me and it's an incredibly selfish, egotistical thing to do and the only person it hurts is the one doing the comparing.

Women are particularly skilled at comparing themselves to and competing with others. I don't see men doing this as often. My husband does not go to work thinking about all the other dudes on the same path and how they're so much better at their jobs than he is and why he's probably just going to suck today. No! He doesn't do that, but we often do. I believe this comparison and competition is so prevalent in women because it's rooted in self-doubt. It's because at the core we doubt our unique gifts and talents. We don't fully love ourselves or see ourselves for the incredible women we were made to be. We overthink our abilities and gifts and then the minute we feel the urge to pursue that thing calling to us in our hearts, we look around to see what everyone else is doing.

I want to let you in on a little secret that changed this all for me, a small flip of the mind that works every time. Today when I see another woman kicking ass in a similar capacity that I desire to kick ass in, I think, "Wow, it's possible and there's opportunity." The fact that someone is making a living pursuing something similar to what I want to do shows me there's a market. That what they have to offer—which is similar to mine (not the same)—is helping people. People are looking for what they offer and maybe if I keep on the path I'm on, there will be people for me too. What if instead of seeing these other women as competition we see them as evidence, proof points that what we're being called to do is valuable?

Think of it this way: when I set out to write this book, I stopped myself many times because I thought, "There are so many books already written, some very similar to the one I want to write." But then I met with my editing team and writing coach and they said to me, "What if there was only one cookbook out there? What if someone wrote a book on French cooking and then everyone who came after them simply didn't write a French cookbook because it had already been done? Wouldn't that be sad?" That helped me understand the need for all sorts of voices and perspectives and stories. We want more than one voice. We need more than one perspective. I had a similar experience one day while I was walking my dog, thinking about others who are on a similar path as mine. As I looked into the woods that surround our house, I took note of all the trees. We live on an old Christmas tree farm so all of the trees, with very few exceptions, are pines. They look similar and taken individually they are pretty, but when you put them all together in a forest, they're breathtaking.

Use others' successes and journeys as evidence, proof that you're on the right path. Your story needs to be shared like my story needs to be shared. Your perspective is different and valuable; don't keep that from the world. We need lots of cookbooks and lots of trees just like we need your gifts. And by pursuing your gifts, you're on the road to living your best life.

Can We Please Stop Saying We Feel Bad?

I've noticed a trend with women lately. It's language we use, a habit we've formed. The habit is the use of the phrase, "I feel bad." We use it in reference to situations involving others, when we need to make a choice. I've heard it used frequently among varying groups of women. They use it as a justification for their actions.

Let me explain. Let's say you're caught between two obligations. There's a work event you want to attend but it happens to fall at the same time as a performance at your child's school. You choose to attend the school performance because that's what important to you and it's where you feel you need to be. Now let's fast forward to a conversation with your friends, family, or colleagues where you find yourself using the phrase, "I feel bad" when describing why you made the choice you made. We need to notice and eliminate our use of this phrase in this context.

Why? Because words and phrases matter and too often as women, we put ourselves in this position of apologizing for our actions rather than owning our decisions. If you're making sound decisions, based on careful consideration of your time and values, there's no need to apologize for them. Think about it: would you ever hear a man say he feels bad for his decision? No, because we all need to make decisions and if we all do the best we can, there's no reason to feel bad. The other thing this phrase does is open the door for criticism from others. When you say you feel bad, others want to help you not feel bad, so they'll give you their opinion and everyone's got one! When we say, "I feel bad," it implies we're not confident in the decision we made because if we were, we wouldn't say we feel bad. Why do we feel bad? Do we actually feel bad or are we just saying it out of routine and habit? My guess is the latter.

This disempowering phrase has become a habit we don't even realize we're doing; we're saying it unconsciously without recognizing how it sounds and the response it receives. This ties into self-love and checking your internal and external dialogue. Words matter. Own your decisions, own your power and stop saying you feel bad.

THE Game Changer of All Game Changers

God has given each of you a gift from His great variety of spiritual gifts. Use them to serve one another. Do you have the gift of speaking? Then speak as though God himself were speaking through you. Do you have the gift of helping others? Do it with all the strength and energy that God supplies. Then everything you do will bring glory to God through Jesus Christ. All glory and power to him forever and ever! Amen.

—1 Peter 4:10-11 NLT

All right, I've saved the very best for very last. You've heard me mention it throughout this book, but I'm going to take the very last pages to spell this out. I want to share with you how faith has radically changed my path. I've saved it until the very end out of respect for anyone who picks up this book and wants to skip this section, but still get all the other nuggets. But if you ask me, you shouldn't skip it even if you don't believe you can relate. I include it because it has been the most radical game changer in my life, and I would be doing you a disservice if I don't discuss it.

I don't care what you believe in, but you must believe in something. There are so many different religions and spiritual-ities in the world, and I respect ones I do not follow. But the only place I can honestly speak from is my personal belief and faith that has changed my life and everything I am called to be and do. That belief is in God. The book you're holding was an assignment from Him. This happened after I had started the book and we went through our housing challenges; I found myself seeking Him and his direction for my life. It was during this time that He started moving in my life and my family in amazing ways.

Since moving twice in twelve months, I have tried to find the purpose for that time and the pain and confusion we lived through. There have been so many good things that have happened as a result of that uncertainty but probably the most significant was the growth in our faith. God moved in such incredible ways during that time and it was the first time we had to fully submit and lay it before Him. Because our plan clearly wasn't working, we turned to Him and asked him to take the wheel. He guided us out of our troubles and put us on the paths we are now, assignments from Him. This book and my path are assignments from Him. I don't worry about the outcome of this book or whether or not it will be successful because it's from Him. That's not to say it will be a success, but the reasons he guided me in this direction are beyond my understanding and I feel tremendous peace in that knowing. I trust Him. I trust His plan for my life, and I choose not to worry.

When I was little, I grew up going to church almost every Sunday, so faith was a part of my life. I also attended a summer bible camp every year until I was eighteen years old. It was at camp that I first experienced God. I knew He existed because I felt it; I had a supernatural connection that I can only describe as an inner knowing. I didn't hear his voice or have any sort of vision, I could just feel him. When I felt him, it felt like the greatest peace, warmth, love, and richness you could ever imagine.

But I haven't always had this faith. And maybe you're in a

stage where you don't have it either; maybe you kept reading because you're curious about how it's helped me build my ideal life. As I grew up, went through school and then started my career, I fell away from the church. I never stopped believing, but I didn't practice my faith. Faith was something I did only by going to church on major holidays. I always knew I wanted to get back, but I didn't make it a priority. That was until I met my friend Anna who introduced me to the Bible study group that followed. Anna and a few other critical players in my life had a peace that I wanted in my life. When I looked at the people who had this peace, they all had one thing in common: faith. I knew God, but I wasn't walking with him at that point in my life, so I found people who could help get me back on track.

Over the past five years I've made faith and my walk with God a top priority and now, it is THE top priority. The way this plays out in my life is through attending church weekly, my weekly Bible study group, daily prayer and meditation, listening to Christian music, and continually seeking Him. My faith has made all the difference in finding and living out my purpose. I couldn't complete this book without at least sharing with you my difference maker. He is the difference maker in my life.

For someone who doesn't believe in God, this all might sound a little "woo woo" and I get it, I've been there. I think what makes it difficult is that it all boils down to faith. It's not something we can see, it's something we feel. We see it lived through other people's lives and actions, but we don't actually experience it unless we believe ourselves. But in most cases, you must take the first steps in belief in order to see or feel it. Faith, in its simplest definition, is putting your complete trust in something you cannot see. Typically, when we think of faith, we think of a supernatural faith, a spiritual or Godly faith, and while that's accurate, it is also believing in the unknown and the unseen. Faith is something we do; it's an action and something we practice.

Stay with me here, but I believe one of the greatest gifts of my spiritual faith is putting into practice my trust in the unknown. Just for a moment we're going to set God aside and discuss the power of faith for the believer. Faith changes the person who's choosing to put their confidence in the unknown. I have observed close friends and business partners who do not have a Godly faith and I've talked with them about their journeys in life and business. They journeys have been noticeably harder, less enjoyable and fraught with fear. Their ability to trust in blind faith is not a skill they've developed, therefore trusting in their journeys is a new practice. What I have observed is that the practice of faith, and it is a practice, changes the person and their ability to put their trust in the unknown. Have you ever thought about that?

When you're building a business and a balanced life, the goals you're working towards are unseen. They can only be seen in the mind and imagined before they become a reality. You're walking in faith when you trust this vision can become a reality. My faith practice has helped me become much more adept at putting my complete trust in what cannot be seen, including in business. Faith changes the believer. And like anything, the more you practice, the better you become.

Practicing your spiritual belief is an area where you also need to develop healthy habits that serve you and your life. Faith is not serving if it's only practiced here and there without dedication or consistent action. In order to truly benefit, it must be something you practice and prioritize daily. This daily practice establishes a habit and establishing healthy habits usually spills over into more habits. It's one more area where we can practice this discipline.

But in the end, my trust in God is what has allowed me to

have total trust in my purpose here on earth and my path. I lived so much of my life trying to control it all. In the first half of my entrepreneurial journey I put my faith in myself and I know how that turned out—I wasn't balanced, I wasn't happy. The second half I put my faith in God and things have been radically smoother. The outcomes have been more fruitful and the journey has been more enjoyable. Peace, love, patience, kindness, and service towards others are now top priorities and business objectives. My desire is to live my life reflecting God's peace and love and I trust that the tasks he lays before me are purposeful and in service to others. Thank you for being a part of this journey with me, I will be praying for you as you walk your respective journeys.

Yes, I am the vine; you are the branches. Those who remain in me, and I in them, will produce much fruit. For apart from me you can do nothing.

—John 15:5 NLT

Journaling Prompts: Putting Pen to Paper and Getting Real

1. What advice would you give to your younger self or someone asking you about how you got to where you are today? If you had to eliminate "hard work" what would you say? Let's stop choosing easy and start being honest about what it takes. If you think it was hard, describe what was hard. For many, it's not the work but rather the mental junk. Let's get intentional about the advice we give.

2. What are your comparison traps? Where do you find yourself getting stuck in the negativity of comparison?

3. What do you need to do to love on yourself and others more?

4. Do you or have you ever used the phrase, "I feel bad"? Has it become a habit? If so, describe how you actually feel. What other things can you say that tell the truth about how you're feeling and give back your power?

Taking the Lesson One Step Further with Recommended Reading

The Bible, the number one selling book for pretty much ever.

One Action Step to Build Momentum

Start a gratitude practice. Every morning write down 5 – 10 things you're thankful for and focus on your blessings for the rest of the day.

Conclusion

THAT'S ALL SHE wrote (for now) . . .

Pursuing the dream to write this book was incredibly exhilarating at times, rich in purpose and growth, as well as terrifying and wrought with fear. There's something about putting your thoughts down in writing for the whole world to read that makes you second guess everything you believe and makes you want to hide under the covers. But I completed it because I knew I had to, this is part of my story. Just like you need to do whatever it is that's on your heart. Don't second guess yourself! Only you know what that thing is.

I know it's scary and you might fail, and people might talk about you behind your back or your friends might not support you. Those are all fears I had when I set out to write this book too. And you know what? It was scary and I did fail many times. (I mean, hello! I tried to build a house in order to avoid doing this and we all know how that turned out.) People did talk about me and some of my closest friends didn't support me. But it's all OK because through this journey I discovered myself and fell in love with me and who I am becoming. I grew in this journey and the people who were attracted to what I was doing started supporting me and coming on board. I've never felt more supported and loved in my entire life.

Each person, including you, is on their own journey. Will this book be a *New York Times* bestseller? I don't know, but it doesn't matter. The end result wasn't why I wrote it. I wrote it because it's part of my purpose; it's part of who I am called to be and what I am called to do. I don't know exactly where the road leads from here but I'm more excited than ever. I'm building the tools, the courage, and the confidence to pursue anything that sets my soul on fire. I will not waste this life or take it for granted and I pray you don't either. We're here on purpose for a purpose; don't stop until you find yours. Just make sure that no matter where you are in your journey, you pursue your dreams in the most balanced way possible. The world needs your gifts but not without your best self. You're a greater gift when you take care of you first.

I hope you learned from my lessons and that you enjoyed reading this book, but I also hope you found yourself saying, "I can totally do this." I hope that if you found parts of the book remarkable, that you also found parts that weren't. Why? Because our shared humanness is both remarkable and yet totally ordinary as well. Some of the most inspiring books, business ideas, podcasts and leaders are the ones that make me kick myself and say, "I could totally do that!" And they did. I hope this book is that for you. I hope there was some wisdom you needed but I also hope it gave you the courage to try, to take the first step and share your gifts with the world.

Lastly, I want you to know that many well-intentioned, protective people throughout my life have tried to tell me it's not possible to have it all, that I should be more realistic. And while I wish them well, I'm so damn thankful I didn't listen to them! Be cautious of the voices you let guide your decisions and actions. Trust your instincts and your heart and soul more than you trust the world. You already possess all of the greatness inside of you to lead an extraordinary, balanced life. Now go do it!

With all the love and encouragement.—Jess

Gratitudes

EVEN THOUGH THIS book has one person's name on the cover, it took a community to birth it into existence. First and foremost, I thank Our Creator, The Big Man Upstairs, for placing this calling into my heart and walking with me through every part of the journey, helping to shape the end result you see today.

I thank my family—my husband John, who supported me and encouraged me to keep going when things were difficult. He watched our kids when I needed to write; he never complained when my alarm went off every morning before sunrise to begin writing, and he believed in me and this vision when I didn't believe it myself. You are my best friend and greatest source of encouragement. I love you. My girls, Wren and Emerson, who from the moment of their births gave me reason to strive for balance in everything I do and stay present because today is all we have. I am grateful for my parents, Don and Jo Ann who instilled countless lessons in me as a girl, always encouraging me to pursue my dreams. My sister, Jen who has always cheered me on—you were my first best friend and you are the one I turn to when I need someone to listen. To Erik, who in his short life taught me the greatest lesson I carry with me every single day: Life is precious, fragile, and unpredictable. It is in your honor that I will not waste my time here on earth. I love you and miss you tremendously.

I am grateful for my writing and support team—Sara Connell and Katie Kizer, you helped create the foundation and structure to get me started and polished my work all along the journey. The success of this book is in large part due to your efforts and contribution, thank you. Kaela Gedda and Brynn Joki, you girls never doubted me and often called B.S. on my excuses. Thank you for pushing me and encouraging me to dream bigger.

My friends and community—I wish I could give credit to every single person who said or sent encouraging words my way through this process via text, Facebook, LinkedIn and Instagram—you can never know the deep impact your words had on me during some of the hardest moments; thank you.

My partners and team—from my very first business partner to the thousands of women who have partnered with me in business since, I thank you all. I couldn't have written this book without the entrepreneurial background I've been blessed to live and each of you has played a role in that success.

Kahlo & Oliver—who kept me company every single day as I wrote this book, life is just more fun with furry, four-legged friends.

Sources

A Look at the Shocking Student Loan Debt Statistics for 2018. Student Loan Hero: May 1, 2018.

https://studentloanhero.com/student-loan-debt-statistics/ Date Accessed: June 2018

Albers Denhart, Chris, Forbes Special Features: *How The $1.2 Trillion College Debt Crisis Is Crippling Students, Parents And The Economy.* Aug 7, 2013.

https://www.forbes.com/sites/specialfeatures/2013/08/07/how-the-college-debt-is-crippling-students-parents-and-the-economy/#88de24d2e171 Date Accessed: June 2018

Alexander, Scott. *Rhinoceros Success: The Secret to Charging Full Speed Toward Every Opportunity.* Tennessee: Ramsey Press, The Lampo Group, 1980.

American Academy of Dermatology | Association. *Skin Conditions by the Numbers.*

https://www.aad.org/media/stats/conditions/skin-conditions-by-the-numbers Date Accessed: September 2018

Andrew, Douglas R., Andrew, Emron D., Andrew, Aaron R. *Millionaire by Thirty: The Quickest Path to Early Financial Independence.* New York: Hachette Book Group, 2008.

Baker, Lisa-Jo. *We Saved You a Seat: Finding and Keeping Lasting Friendships*. Nashville, TN: LifeWay Press, 2017.

Brodsky, Norm and Burlingham, Bo. *The Knack: How Street-Smart Entrepreneurs Learn to Handle Whatever Comes Up*. New York: Penguin Books, 2008.

Burchard, Brendon. *High Performance Habits: How Extraordinary People Become That Way*. Unites States: Hay House, 2017.

Chatzky, Jean. *The Difference: How Anyone Can Prosper in Even the Toughest Times*. New York: Penguin Random House, 2009.

Collins, Jim. *Good to Great: Why Some Companies Make the Leap...and Others Don't*. New York: HarperCollins, 2001.

Dweck, Carol. *Mindset: the New Psychology of Success*. Audiobooks, 2008.

DeWolf, Mark. *12 Stats About Working Women*. U.S. Department of Labor Blog: March 1, 2017.

https://blog.dol.gov/2017/03/01/12-stats-about-working-women Date Accessed: June 2018

Ferris, Timothy. *The 4-Hour Workweek: Escape 9-5, Live Anywhere, and Join the New Rich (Expanded and Updated)*. Audiobooks, 2000.

Grabinowski, Ed. *How Social Security Works*. https://money.howstuffworks.com/personal-finance/financial-planning/social-security4.htm Date Accessed: June 2018

Hill, Napoleon. *Think and Grow Rich*. Audiobook: 2000.

Huffington, Arianna. *The Sleep Revolution: Transforming Your Life, One Night at a Time*. New York: Harmony Books, 2016.

Hunter, James C. *The Servant: A Simple Story About The True Essence of Leadership.* New York: Crown Publishing Group, 2012.

Life Without Limbs // Nick Vujicic. https://www.lifewithout limbs.org. Date Accessed: July 2018.

Maxwell, John. *Winning is an Inside Job.* The John Maxwell Leadership Podcast. June 25, 2018. iTunes Podcast.

Maxwell, John C. *How Successful People Think: Change Your Thinking, Change Your Life.* New York: Hachette Book Group, 2009.

Maxwell, John C. *The 15 Invaluable Laws of Growth: Live Them and Reach Your Potential.* New York: Hachette Book Group, 2012.

Merriam-Webster: https://www.merriam-webster.com/dictio nary/entrepreneur. Date Accessed: May 2018.

Olson, Jeff. *The Slight Edge: Turning Simple Disciplines into Massive Success & Happiness.* Texas: SUCCESS, 2005-2013.

Pink, Daniel H. *To Sell is Human: The Surprising Truth About Moving Others.* Audiobooks, 2012.

Pink, Daniel H. *Why extroverts fail, introverts flounder and you probably succeed.* January 28, 2013. The Washington Post: https://www.washingtonpost.com/national/on-leadership/ why-extroverts-fail-introverts-flounder-and-you- probably-succeed/2013/01/28/bc4949b0-695d-11e2- 95b3-272d604a10a3_story.html?noredirect=on&utm_ term=.8275089bfd7b Date Accessed: September 2018

Robbins, Mel. *Stop Saying You're Fine: Discover a More Powerful You.* New York: Random House, 2011.

Robbins, Mel. *The 5 Second Rule.* Audiobooks, 2017.

Sincero, Jen. *You are a Badass: How to Stop Doubting Your Greatness and Start Living an Awesome Life.* Pennsylvania: Running Press, 2013.

Sincero, Jen. *You are a Badass at Making Money: Master the Mindset of Wealth.* Great Britain: John Murray Learning: 2017.

Sharma, Robin. *The Monk Who Sold His Ferrari: A Spiritual Fable About Fulfilling Your Dreams and Reaching Your Destiny.* Audiobooks, 2007.

Stanny, Barbara. *Secrets of Six-Figure Women: Surprising Strategies to up Your Earnings and Change Your Life.* New York: HarperCollins, 2004.

Tómasdóttir, Halla: *How Can Leaders Inspire Others To Lead?.* TED Radio Hour: https://www.npr.org/templates/transcript/transcript.php?storyId=612159658 Date Accessed: May 2018

Tómasdóttir, Halla: *It's Time for Women to Run for Office.* TEDWomen2016:

https://www.ted.com/talks/halla_tomasdottir_it_s_time_for_women_to_run_for_office. Date Accessed: May 2018

Vinton, Kate. *How Two Dermatologists Built A Billion Dollar Brand In Their Spare Time.* Forbes: June 21, 2016. https://www.forbes.com/sites/katevinton/2016/06/01/billion-dollar-brand-proactiv-rodan-fields/#6218953b3bfe Date Accessed: September 2018

Wikipedia: https://en.wikipedia.org/wiki/Personal_development. Date Accessed: July 2018.

Wikipedia: https://en.wikipedia.org/wiki/Nick_Vujicic. Date Accessed: July 2018.

Wikipedia: https://en.wikipedia.org/wiki/Under_the_Tuscan_Sun_(film). Date Accessed: August 2018.